2ND EDITION
WORKBOOK

T0350664

Contents

1 All About School

1 What school activities do you see in the pictures? Write the numbers.

1
2
3
4
5
6

___ **a** going on a field trip   ___ **b** giving a presentation

___ **c** working on computers   ___ **d** taking a test

___ **e** doing a project   ___ **f** handing in an assignment

2 Read and ✓. What would you like your school to have?

	lots of	some	none
1 free time	☐	☐	☐
2 homework	☐	☐	☐
3 tests	☐	☐	☐
4 group projects	☐	☐	☐
5 after-school clubs	☐	☐	☐
6 independent work	☐	☐	☐
7 field trips	☐	☐	☐
8 computers	☐	☐	☐

3 ✓ the verbs you use with each phrase. Then listen and check your answers.

	do	study for	hand in	finish
1 a test				
2 an assignment				
3 a book report				
4 homework				
5 a project				

4 Read. Match the name with the excuse. Write the letter.

Katherine — I finished my essay, but

Mark — I can't hand in my book report because

Tabitha — I couldn't finish my history project

Dean — I wanted to study for the math test, but

___ **1** Katherine

___ **2** Mark

___ **3** Tabitha

___ **4** Dean

a I started playing video games and ran out of time.

b I left my book on the bus yesterday.

c because I didn't start until yesterday.

d my puppy ate it when I wasn't looking.

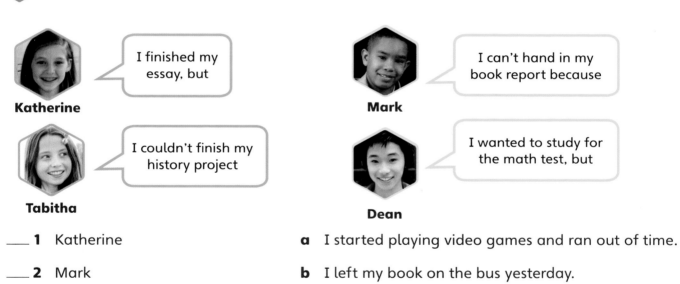

THINK BIG

Complete the sentences with an excuse or some advice.

1 A: Ben hasn't finished his science project because he didn't start it until last night.

B: He _____.

2 A: Rich _____.

B: He should have been more careful.

How did I do? ☆☆☆☆☆

5 Listen and read. Circle **T** for true or **F** for false.

ninja_fly

Hi, everyone! What's going on? I need your advice. I have this problem with my mom. My mom has volunteered for every dance, every field trip, and every fundraising activity we've had at school so far this year. Sometimes I like it. But you know something? Children make fun of me because she's always here. It's embarrassing. I know she thinks the school needs her help, but I need her help, too... to stay away. What should I do?

free_mind09

OK, ninja_fly. I understand you. It can be really annoying to have your mom at school all the time. You should tell her how you feel. Ask her to stop volunteering for everything and stop coming to school so often. Take my advice. I had the same problem with my mom and it worked for me.

2good_for_u

I agree with free_mind09. You should tell your mom that it bothers you when she comes to school so often. But I don't think she should stop volunteering. I'll bet she likes it and the school needs it. You should be glad she wants to help. You should tell her that she's a brilliant mom, but that you would like her to volunteer at school less often. Think positively!

1   Ninja_fly's mom volunteers too much at his school.   T   F

2   Both free_mind09 and 2good_for_u think ninja_fly   T   F
    should tell his mom to stop volunteering so much.

3   Free_mind09 didn't have the same problem with her mom.   T   F

4   2good_for_u thinks volunteering is good.   T   F

6   Answer the question.

If your mom volunteered at your school, would you feel the same way as ninja_fly?
Why/Why not?

_____

_____

How did I do?

Language in Action

7 **Listen and read. Circle the correct answers.**

Jim: Hey, Ollie. Have you met the new exchange student yet?

Ollie: No. Why?

Jim: She's from Finland and she's really nice!

Ollie: Nice, <u>huh</u>? Is she smart, too?

Jim: Very smart. I've talked to her in English. But maybe I'll start learning Finnish now.

Ollie: <u>You're crazy</u>. You haven't even learned English yet and you *are* English.

Jim: Finnish is different. I'm sure I'll learn it fast. I'm motivated!

Ollie: <u>Yeah, yeah, yeah.</u>

1 Ollie **has seen / hasn't seen** the exchange student.

2 Jim **has already talked / hasn't talked** to the exchange student.

3 The exchange student **speaks / doesn't speak** English.

8 **Look at 7. Circle the correct answers.**

1 When Ollie says, "Nice, huh?", "huh" means that he's

    a not interested.   **b** interested.

2 "You're crazy" means

    a what you're saying doesn't make any sense. **b** what you're saying makes sense.

3 The expression "yeah, yeah, yeah" means

    a I like what you say.   **b** I don't believe that you'll do what you say.

9 **Circle the correct expression. Then listen and check.**

1 **A:** I'm going to stop playing video games forever!

    B: **Huh? / You're crazy!** You've played video games ever since I met you.

2 **A:** Jeffrey hasn't asked anyone to the dance yet.

    B: He hasn't, **yeah, yeah, yeah. / huh?** I wonder who he'll ask.

3 **A:** This time I'm going to hand in my project on time.

    B: **You're crazy! / Yeah, yeah, yeah.** That's what you always say!

How did I do? ☆☆☆☆☆

Grammar

Has she **done** her solo <u>yet</u>?	Yes, she **has**. She **has** <u>already</u> **done** it. No, she **hasn't**. She **hasn't done** it <u>yet</u>.
Have they <u>ever</u> **won** an award?	Yes, they **have**. No, they **haven't**.

10 **Read about Michael and Ted. Then write the answers or questions.**

Michael and Ted's Social Studies Project

 Michael and Ted are playing video games. They haven't started their social studies project.

 Michael has finished making the model pyramid, but Ted hasn't finished his research yet.

 Michael and Ted have finished their project. Ted has fallen asleep.

1 It's 8:45 p.m. Have Michael and Ted gotten supplies for their project yet?

<u>Yes, they have. They've already gotten supplies for their project.</u>

2 It's 8:45 p.m. Has Michael completed the model of the pyramid yet?

_____

3 It's 2:00 a.m. Has Ted started doing research on the computer yet?

_____

4 It's 8:15 a.m. _____

Yes, they have. Michael and Ted have already arrived in class.

5 It's 8:30 a.m. _____

Yes, they have. Michael and Ted have handed in their project.

How did I do? ☆ ☆ ☆ ☆ ☆

He **has** <u>already</u> **finished** the project.   He **finished** it <u>yesterday</u>.
He **hasn't finished** the project <u>yet</u>.   He **didn't finish** it <u>yesterday</u>.

11   **Look at Sarita's to-do list. Then complete the sentences.**

1 Sarita _____made_____ posters for the art fair at 4:00.

2 She _____has_____ already _____made_____ posters for the art fair.

3 Sarita _____ her book report at 5:30.

4 She _____ already _____ her book report.

5 Sarita _____ her science project yet.

6 Sarita _____ her science project tonight.

Things to do:

1 Make posters for art
fair at 4:00 ✓

2 Start book report
at 5:30 ✓

3 Finish science project
tonight ◯

12   **Complete the dialogs. Use the correct form of the verbs
in parentheses.**

1 **A:** Has Manuel _____ (do) the laundry yet?

    B: No, he _____ the laundry yet.

2 **A:** Has Trudie _____ (hand in) her homework yet?

    B: No, she _____ her homework yet.

3 **A:** Has Sean _____ (eat) dinner yet?

    B: Yes, he _____ dinner at 6:00.

13   **Circle the correct form of the verb.**

1 I **have finished** / **finished** my assignment last night, but I **haven't handed** / **didn't
hand** it in yet.

2 Jan **has already taken** / **took** the test yesterday, but she **has studied** / **didn't study** for
it. She forgot there was a test.

3 We **haven't started** / **didn't start** our project yet. We **haven't had** / **didn't have** time
yesterday.

15

14 Read and complete. Then listen and check.

| on average | according to | behavior | published | depressed |

Do you get enough sleep?

The American Academy of Sleep **1**_____ a report in 2016. **2**_____ the report, teens 13–18 years old should sleep 8–10 hours a day. If teens don't get enough sleep, they can become **3**_____ or have **4**_____ problems. Studies show that, **5**_____, teens don't get enough sleep.

15 Did they get enough sleep last night? Read and circle **Y** for yes or **N** for no.

What time did you go to bed? What time did you get up?

Did you get enough sleep last night?

1
I went to bed at 11 p.m. last night and I got up at 6 a.m. I had an assignment to do, but I didn't understand it. I was talking to my friend in class when the teacher was explaining. That's why it took me a long time to do.
Y N

2
I was so tired and sleepy that I went to bed at 9 p.m. after I watched an hour of TV. I got up at 7 a.m. this morning and went for a run.
Y N

3
I was just about to finish my English homework and go to bed when I pressed the wrong button on my computer. I lost my homework and I had to start again. I went to bed at 1 a.m. this morning and I got up at 8 a.m.
Y N

4
I watched a great soccer game last night. After it finished at 10 p.m., I started my homework, which took an hour. I got up at 6 a.m.
Y N

16 Look at **15**. Write advice for the teens who didn't get enough sleep last night.

You should have _____ .
_____
_____

How did I do? ☆ ☆ ☆ ☆ ☆

17 **Listen and read. Then complete the chart.**

Differences in Education

All around the world, children go to school. Yet, education in one country may be very different than education in another country. Schools may differ in the number of hours that students spend there every day. They may also be different in the subjects that students can study, or the pace with which they move through the curriculum.

Education in Finland, China, and Poland is different in some ways, but students in all these countries do well on achievement tests. Finland has the highest scores in science, math, and reading, yet students go to school for only four hours a day, on average. That's quite amazing! Most students in Poland are at school a little longer. In China, children are in school from 8 to 11 hours a day.

Class size is also different. In Finland, classes are small. The average class size is 18. Classes in Poland have about 25 students. In China, they're much larger. The way the school day is structured is different, too. Students in China and Poland follow schedules, but in Finland, students decide what they want to do each day. The teacher gives them practical choices and the students decide.

Students in these countries don't do a lot of homework. Is homework important? People have very different opinions on this topic. The interesting thing is that students in these countries learn a lot without doing a lot of homework or memorizing facts. They have more time to enjoy learning about things outside the classroom, or to do hobbies. Do you think that's the reason their test scores are so high?

	Finland	China	Poland
How many hours of school?	4	1 _____	4–5
How large are classes?	2 _____	37	3 _____
Is there a schedule?	4 _____	5 _____	Yes

18 **Read 17 again and circle T for true or F for false.**

1   Students in Finland do well on achievement tests.   T   F

2   Children in China spend more time at school than children in Poland.   T   F

3   Class size is the largest in Poland.   T   F

4   Students in Finland have a strict school schedule.   T   F

5   Children in Finland do more homework than children in China.   T   F

How did I do? ☆ ☆ ☆ ☆ ☆

In an opinion paragraph, you share your opinion about a topic. To write an opinion paragraph, follow these steps:

- Write your opinion. Use your opinion as the title of your opinion paragraph. For example: *Longer School Days Will Not Improve Grades*

- To begin your opinion paragraph, rewrite the title of your paragraph as a question. Then answer the question with your opinion:
Will longer school days improve grades? In my opinion, they won't.

- Next, write reasons for your opinion:
Students will be too tired after a longer school day to do their homework. They'll have less time to work on school projects and study for tests.

- Then, write suggestions:
I think offering after-school study periods for students who need extra help is a better idea. Teachers could also organize more group projects. That way, students could help each other while they complete assignments.

- Finally, write a conclusion:
In my opinion, offering extra help to students and organizing more group projects are better ideas than having longer school days. Longer school days might even cause students to get even lower grades because they'll be tired and more stressed.

19   **Choose one of the school issues below. Write your opinion.**

- Students **should** / **shouldn't** use cell phones at school.

- It's **important** / **not important** to use computers in the classroom.

My opinion: _____

20   **Write an outline for your topic in 19. Complete the chart.**

Title rewritten as question:	
Main opinion:	
Reason:	
Suggestion:	
Conclusion:	

21   **Write an opinion paragraph on a separate piece of paper. Use your notes from 20.**

How did I do? ☆ ☆ ☆ ☆ ☆

Review

22 **Read about Anna's day. Use the words to write questions. Then write the answers.**

DONE
do my social studies homework

Anna

NOT DONE
study for math test

1 yet / Anna / do / social studies homework

Q: _____

A: _____

2 study for / math test / her / she / yet

Q: _____

A: _____

23 **Complete the sentences. Use the correct form of the verbs in parentheses.**

1 Mark _____ (not study) for his math test yesterday.

2 Sarah _____ (not finish) her book report last week.

3 Juan _____ (not hand in) his history assignment yet.

4 Marissa _____ (not do) her homework yet.

24 **Look at 23. Write excuses using the ideas in the box.**

| lost the book   forgot about it   ran out of time   the dog ate it |

1 He _didn't study for the test because he forgot about it._____

2 She _____

3 He _____

4 She _____

How did I do? ☆☆☆☆☆

2 Amazing Young People

1 Match the pictures with the sentences about life dreams. Write the numbers.

1
2
3
4
5
6

Someday I would like to…

___ **a** create a photography blog.

___ **b** start my own band.

___ **c** be a professional soccer player.

___ **d** volunteer in Africa.

___ **e** climb a mountain.

___ **f** find a cure for diseases.

2 Write down four of your dreams and rank them:
1 = most important, 4 = least important.

1 _____

2 _____

3 _____

4 _____

3 Look at 2. Which dream will be the most difficult to achieve? Draw a box around it. Which dream will be the easiest to achieve? Underline it. Which dream can you achieve right now? Write it here:

_____

4 **Read. Then circle T for true or F for false.**

My parents are amazing people! My mom's a writer. She wrote and published her first book when she was just 14 years old! She also speaks three languages: English, Spanish, and French. My dad is a famous chess player. He has played chess for over 20 years and has won many tournaments. He also plays the piano and the guitar. My parents are amazing people for all their achievements – especially for being wonderful parents to me and my sister!

Our children are amazing! Our son Chris is great at science. At just ten years old, he started his own science club. The club meets every Friday after school. Last week, he won an award for his latest invention: a portable MP3 case that protects your MP3 player from getting wet! He wants to be a doctor when he grows up. Emma's a terrific athlete! She's the captain of her track and soccer teams. Her soccer team has just won a big soccer tournament. Emma won the Most Valuable Player award! Emma loves being active... her biggest dream is to climb a mountain one day. We are very proud of our amazing children.

1	Chris's dad has published a book.	T	F
2	His mom speaks three languages.	T	F
3	Chris's dad plays two instruments.	T	F
4	Chris hasn't invented anything yet.	T	F
5	Emma's team has just won a soccer tournament.	T	F
6	Emma has already climbed a mountain.	T	F

5 **Complete the sentences. Use the words in the box.**

invented something   published a book   speak 23 languages   won a tournament

1 Harry, a young boy from Hampshire, U.K., _____ called *Junior Bake Off*. He won with his amazing carrot cake.

2 Kevin Doe _____ amazing when he was only 13. He made batteries from junk and helped bring electricity to people's homes in Sierra Leone.

3 Timothy Donor taught himself to _____ by the time he was 16.

4 Adora Svitak _____ about how to write when she was only 7.

Which of the achievements in 5 do you think is the most important? Why?

How did I do? ☆☆☆☆☆

6 **Listen and read. Then answer the questions.**

Adora Svitak

by Tracy Dorington

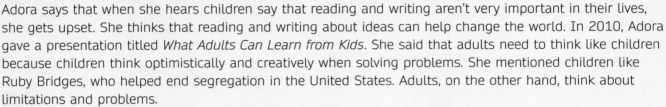

Adora Svitak considers herself a writer, a teacher, and an activist. She began writing when she was four years old. She wrote *Flying Fingers* at age seven. In it, she talks about how important writing is and explains how to write. In 2008, Adora published a book of poetry that she co-wrote with her sister.

Adora says that when she hears children say that reading and writing aren't very important in their lives, she gets upset. She thinks that reading and writing about ideas can help change the world. In 2010, Adora gave a presentation titled *What Adults Can Learn from Kids*. She said that adults need to think like children because children think optimistically and creatively when solving problems. She mentioned children like Ruby Bridges, who helped end segregation in the United States. Adults, on the other hand, think about limitations and problems.

Adora continues to publish her work and give speeches. In 2011, she published her first full-length novel, *Yang in Disguise*. In 2012, Adora won an award given by the National Press Club. At the awards ceremony, she gave a speech about the importance of girls achieving their goals and living their dreams. One of Adora's goals is to win a Nobel Prize.

Adora believes that the way to change the world is to trust children and expect that they'll do great things at a young age. Parents and teachers, she says, have low expectations of students. They don't expect children to achieve much. They expect children to listen and not show their brilliance. This thinking has to change. She says that adults should expect wonderful things and learn to listen to children. The future depends on it.

1 What's one of Adora's accomplishments?

_____

2 What's one of Adora's future goals?

_____

3 How does Adora believe the world should change?

_____

4 Do you agree or disagree with Adora? Explain your answer.

_____

_____

How did I do? ☆ ☆ ☆ ☆ ☆

Language in Action

28
7 Listen and read. Circle T for true or F for false.

Jen: Phil, what's your brother doing on his computer? I can see he's really <u>getting into it</u>.

Phil: He's probably working on one of his computer programs.

Jen: He writes computer programs? But he's only twelve!

Phil: I know. He started writing programs when he was about nine.

Jen: Nine? That's incredible!

Phil: He's in trouble with my parents though. He wants to <u>drop out</u> of school and work on his programs all day.

Jen: <u>You're joking</u>, aren't you?

Phil: Yeah, I'm <u>just kidding</u>.

1 Phil's brother likes computers a lot.	T	F
2 His brother started working with computers when he was 12.	T	F
3 Jen isn't interested.	T	F
4 Phil's brother is going to stop going to school.	T	F

8 Look at **7**. Read the underlined expressions. Match the expressions with their meanings. Write the letters.

____ **1** get into

____ **2** drop out

____ **3** be joking

____ **4** be kidding

a say something funny to make people laugh

b say something surprising that doesn't sound possible

c stop going before you finish

d become interested in

9 Answer the questions.

1 Have you ever dropped out of anything? What was it? Why did you drop out?

_____

2 Are you getting into something interesting this year? What is it? Why do you like it?

_____

3 Look at **7**. Why did Jen say, "You're joking"?

_____

How did I do? ☆☆☆☆☆

Grammar

How long **has** she **played** the piano?
She**'s played** the piano <u>for</u> five years.
How long **have** they **known** about William Kamkwamba?
They**'ve known** about him <u>since</u> they saw a movie about him.

10 **Look and match the phrases with since or for.**

11 **Complete the sentences. Use the present perfect form of the verbs in parentheses and for or since.**

1 Karine loves to dance. She _____ (dance) competitively
_____ she was five.

2 Ray loves to read. He _____ (read) two books about the Middle Ages
_____ he learned about it in his social studies class.

3 My dad loves soccer. He _____ (play) soccer every Saturday
_____ thirty years.

4 My mom loves animals. She _____ (work) at the animal shelter
_____ six years.

How did I do? ☆ ☆ ☆ ☆ ☆

> How long **has** your brother **been playing** tennis?
> He**'s been playing** tennis <u>since</u> he was five.
> How long **have** you and your sister **been bungee jumping**?
> We**'ve been bungee jumping** <u>for</u> two years.

12   **Read. Answer the questions. Use the present perfect progressive.**

At age 12, Bobby and Jenny have their own business. They started working at their business, called Kids Biz, when they were nine. They do chores like mowing the grass and washing cars. Six months ago, Jenny started babysitting, too. They also volunteer in the community. Bobby started collecting money for the animal shelter two years ago. He does that every year. Jenny collects food for the homeless. She started doing that when she was 11. They both blog, too. They started blogging when they started sixth grade.

1   How long have Bobby and Jenny been working at Kids Biz?

They have been working at Kids Biz since they were nine.   (since)

2   How long has Jenny been babysitting?

_____ (for)

3   How long has Bobby been collecting money for the animal shelter?

_____ (for)

4   How long has Jenny been collecting food for the homeless?

_____ (since)

5   How long have they been blogging?

_____ (since)

13   **Answer the questions in complete sentences.**

1   Think of something you are studying in school. How long have you been studying it?

_____

2   Think of something you love to do. How long have you been doing it?

_____

How did I do? ☆☆☆☆☆

14 Match the words with the definitions. Write the letters.

___ **1** gifted

___ **2** composed

___ **3** exceptional

___ **4** symphony

___ **5** inspiration

a a long piece of music written for an orchestra

b unusually good

c something that gives you a great idea

d having a natural ability to do something very well

e wrote a piece of music, poem, speech, etc.

15 Read and complete with the words from **14**. Then listen and check.

30

GIFTED CHILDREN

Many children are talented, but some have ¹_____ abilities that make them famous throughout history. Here are just a few examples of ²_____ children who achieved amazing accomplishments when they were still young:

- Wolfgang Amadeus Mozart ³_____ a ⁴_____ at eight, and an opera at fourteen – all by himself!
- At two years old, Aelita Andre created beautiful paintings that art critics through the ages will admire.
- Fourteen-year-old Nadia Comăneci scored a perfect 10 in gymnastics at the Olympic Games – an amazing accomplishment for such a young athlete. As a result, she has become a legend in the world of gymnastics!
- Another talented child, twelve-year-old Louis Braille from France, changed the world of reading and writing forever when he invented the Braille code to help the blind read and write.
Mozart, Andre, Comăneci, and Braille are an ⁵_____ for many people to try to achieve great things!

16 Read **15** again and circle the correct word.

1 Mozart composed **a symphony** / **an opera** when he was fourteen.

2 When she was **two** / **twelve**, Aelita Andre created beautiful paintings.

3 Nadia Comăneci scored a perfect 10 in **diving** / **gymnastics**.

4 The twelve-year-old Louis Braille came from **Portugal** / **France**.

How did I do? ☆☆☆☆☆

17 **Listen and read. What is the purpose of Earthdance International?**

Imagine a World of **Peace**

Conflict happens everywhere. It happens in our homes, our schools, our friendships, and, certainly, in our world. When conflict happens, people start to "take sides". *To take sides* means to believe that one person, group, or opinion is completely right and the others are completely wrong. When people take sides, they often don't listen or hear the other side's opinions or concerns. Do you sometimes feel that someone isn't listening to you when you give your opinion or explain your ideas? How can you encourage people to really listen to you?

Can you imagine a world without conflict? Can you imagine a world where people live together peacefully? Earthdance International can. Earthdance International is an organization that was founded in 1997. Its purpose is to use music and dance to bring people and countries together for peace – especially countries taking sides against each other. Once a year, Earthdance International organizes the Global Festival for Peace. The festival takes place in different countries around the world, at the same time, on the same day. It's "the largest global synchronized music and peace event in the world". It has taken place in over 80 countries, as well as online! Musicians, singers, dancers, and artists from around the world come together to create song and dance. Journalists and representatives from many organizations talk about peaceful ways to end conflict, injustice, and environmental problems. Everyone enjoys the music and fun, but they're also hard at work discussing ways to make the world a better place. Everyone feels that being neutral to difficult problems is the first step toward success in finding peaceful solutions for them.

What would you rather have – conflict or peace? What can you do to make your home, school, neighborhood, or country more peaceful? When you next face a difficult situation, can you think of a peaceful solution?

18 **Complete the sentences with the words in the box.**

conflict	neutral	organization	peace

1 Earthdance International is an _____ that brings people and countries together for peace.

2 Earthdance International believes being _____ is the first step towards peace.

3 People often don't listen when there is _____.

4 There are many people around the world who are working hard to create _____ in difficult areas.

How did I do?

In a biography, you write about the important events and details of someone's life. These can include:

- the place where someone was born
- the schools the person went to and what he or she studied
- the jobs the person had

- accomplishments
- important memories and people
- interests

It helps to ask questions and put the events in the correct order.

19 **Unscramble the questions. Imagine you are interviewing Stephen Hillenburg, the creator of *SpongeBob SquarePants*.**

1 were / where / you / born?

You: _____ ?

Stephen: I was born in Anaheim, California, in 1961.

2 what / study / you / did / in college?

You: _____ ?

Stephen: I studied Marine Biology in college, but I really wanted to study Art.

I got a Master of Fine Arts degree in animation in 1991.

3 are / some / your / what / of / important memories?

You: _____ ?

Stephen: When I was young, I loved watching films about the sea. I loved drawing and painting, too.

4 what / your / some of / are / accomplishments?

You: _____ ?

Stephen: I've made many films but my biggest accomplishment is creating the cartoon *SpongeBob SquarePants* in 1999. In 2013, it won favorite cartoon of the year at the Kids' Choice Awards.

20 **Write a short biography of Stephen Hillenburg. Use the information in 19. Write two more questions. Do research and find the answers. Add the information to the biography.**

How did I do? ☆ ☆ ☆ ☆ ☆

Review

21 **Complete the paragraphs. Use the present perfect and for or since.**

I have some amazing friends.

I ¹_____ (know) my friend Anthony ²_____ we were five years old. He ³_____ (play) chess ⁴_____ 12 years, and he ⁵_____ (win) many tournaments.
I ⁶_____ (try) to beat him at a game
⁷_____ many years, but I ⁸_____ (not have) any luck! Besides being an amazing chess player, Anthony can also speak French! He wants to write and publish a book in French when he's older.

I ⁹_____ (be) friends with Stella ¹⁰_____
three years. She is an amazing musician. She ¹¹_____
(play) the piano ¹²_____ she was four years old. She also loves science.
She ¹³_____ (be) a member of our school's science club
¹⁴_____ over two years. She wants to invent something one day!

I am so lucky to have such amazing friends!

22 **Look at 21. Answer the questions in complete sentences.**

1 Who has won a tournament? _____

2 Who plays an instrument? _____

3 Who speaks another language? _____

4 Who wants to invent something? _____

5 Who wants to write a book? _____

23 **Answer the questions. Use the present perfect progressive and since.**

1 *SpongeBob SquarePants* started in 1999. How long has it been playing on TV?

_____

2 Seeds of Peace started in 1993. How long has Seeds of Peace been training students?

_____

How did I do? ☆☆☆☆☆

Unit 2 **21**

3 Dilemmas

Language in Context

1 Look at the pictures. How do you think the people are feeling? Write the number or numbers.

1   2   3

4   5   6

___ **a** angry   ___ **b** worried   ___ **c** upset

___ **d** guilty   ___ **e** happy   ___ **f** in trouble

___ **g** good about himself
       or herself

2 Look at 1. What do you think has happened to the people? Why do they look this way? Choose one person and ✓ all possible answers. Add three ideas of your own.

The person…

☐ cheated in a test.   ☐ heard a hurtful lie.

☐ helped a friend at school. ☐ stopped a bully.

☐ had a fight with a friend. ☐ _____.

☐ _____.   ☐ _____.

3 Complete the dialogs. Circle the correct words.

1 Kate: Yesterday, I borrowed my mom's jacket, but I lost it at the park. I don't want her to **get into trouble / be upset** with me, so I'm going to tell her that someone else took it.

Sally: Why don't you check the lost property office? Maybe someone found the jacket and took it there. Then you can **feel guilty / tell the truth** and **feel good / return** the jacket to your mom.

2 Jim: My mom asked me who took the money that was on the table. I told her my little brother took it. And now he's going to **tell the truth / get into trouble** and I don't **feel guilty / feel good about** it.

Sam: You should tell your mom the truth, Jim. If you tell the truth, it'll be OK. And tell your brother that you're sorry. But who took the money?

Jim: I don't know.

4 Read the dilemma. What do you think? Complete the sentences. Use your own ideas.

You and your friend find an expensive jacket at the bus stop. There's a wallet in the pocket with an address in it. Your friend takes the jacket and returns it to the owner. The owner gives your friend a reward of $50. Your friend keeps the money and doesn't say anything to you. Then you find out the truth.

1 How do you feel?

I _____.

2 How should your friend feel?

My friend _____.

3 How do you think your friend feels?

My friend probably _____.

4 What should your friend have done?

My friend should have _____.

THINK BIG

Have you had a dilemma recently? What was it? How did you feel? What happened in the end?

_____

_____

How did I do? ☆☆☆☆☆

5 Listen and read. Circle the correct answers.

Gary's Dilemma

Gary was walking out of school when his best friend Ryan ran up to him. "We're OK, right? If my mom calls you, you'll say it's true that I'm studying with you, right?" he whispered. Behind Ryan stood Max and a gang of boys Gary didn't want to know.

Gary nodded, trying to smile.

"Come on, Ryan, let's go!" Max called.

"Just a sec!" Ryan said. He turned back to Gary. "Thanks, Gary. See you soon, OK?"

"Yeah, sure," said Gary, and he turned and headed for home. He should have said no in the first place.

"Hey, Gary! Wait!" Gary turned and saw Pete running towards him.

"Hi, Pete," said Gary, without looking at Pete.

"What's up with you?" Pete said.

"Sorry," said Gary, "I'm just thinking about something."

"By the way," Pete said, "what's up with Ryan? What's he doing hanging out with Max and those other guys? That gang's always getting into trouble!"

"I don't know, but he can do whatever he wants," shrugged Gary.

Pete grabbed Gary's shoulder. "I can't believe you said that! Ryan's our friend. If he's in trouble, we should help him."

Gary looked down, thinking, *If I tell, Ryan will think he can't trust me and I might lose him as a friend. I don't want to be in trouble with the gang, either. But if I don't tell, something terrible might happen to Ryan.* Gary had to make a decision.

1 Ryan and Gary **are** / **aren't** going to study together.

2 Gary **is** / **isn't** going to tell a lie to Ryan's mom.

3 Max and his gang **are** / **aren't** friends of Gary's.

4 Pete thinks he and Gary **have to** / **don't have to** do something to help Ryan.

6 Answer the questions. Use your own ideas.

1 Why do children join gangs? Why do you think Ryan joined the gang?

_____

2 What should Gary and Pete do?

_____

How did I do? ☆ ☆ ☆ ☆ ☆

Language in Action

7 **Listen and read. Then answer the questions.**

Mom: <u>What's the matter</u>, Chris?

Chris: Nothing, Mom.

Mom: Did something happen at school today?

Chris: Well, yeah... but it's not important.

Mom: <u>Look</u>. If you don't tell me what's wrong, I won't be able to help you. Tell me <u>what's going on</u>.

Chris: Well, a couple of boys at school are <u>being mean</u> to me.

Mom: Are they? Did they hurt you?

Chris: No, it's nothing like that. They just <u>call me names</u> sometimes.

Mom: I'm glad you told me, Chris. Let's think about what you can do.

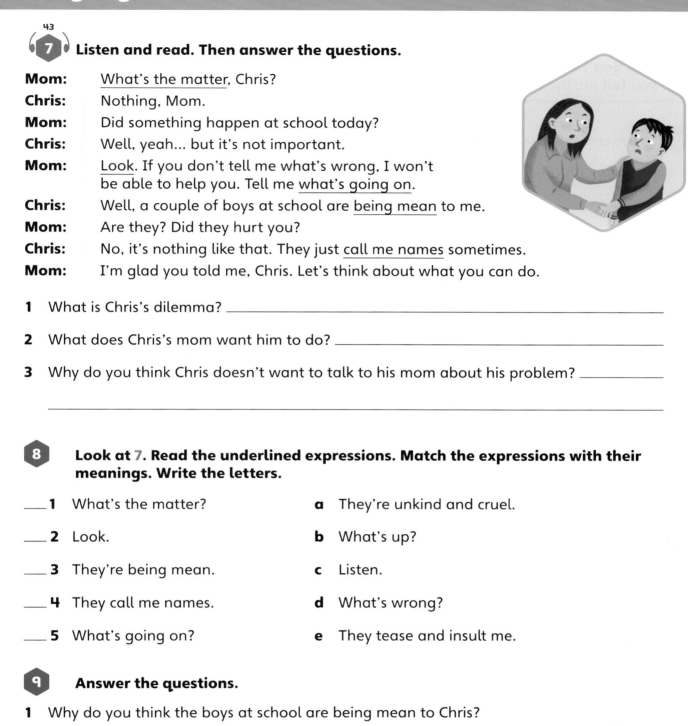

1 What is Chris's dilemma? _____

2 What does Chris's mom want him to do? _____

3 Why do you think Chris doesn't want to talk to his mom about his problem? _____

_____

8 **Look at 7. Read the underlined expressions. Match the expressions with their meanings. Write the letters.**

___**1** What's the matter?

___**2** Look.

___**3** They're being mean.

___**4** They call me names.

___**5** What's going on?

a They're unkind and cruel.

b What's up?

c Listen.

d What's wrong?

e They tease and insult me.

9 **Answer the questions.**

1 Why do you think the boys at school are being mean to Chris?

_____

2 What would you say to someone if he or she called you names?

_____

How did I do?

Grammar

If he **pays attention** in class, he**'ll understand** the lesson.
If they **don't study** for the math test, they **won't get** a good grade.
If you **tell** me the truth, I**'ll help** you.

I can't be late!

10 **Unscramble the phrases to complete the sentences.**

1 (am / late / for / If / I / school)
 If I'm late for school_____, I'll have to go to the office and get
 a late pass.

2 (friend Jimmy / see / I / my / will)
 If I go to the office, _____. He's always late.

3 (see / if / my friend Jimmy / I)
 _____, we'll start talking about manga comics because
 we always do.

4 (will / going back / forget about / we / to our classroom)
 If we start talking about manga comics, _____.

5 (yell / the principal / at us / will)
 _____ if he sees us talking in the hallway.

6 (a / is / he / bad mood / if / in)
 _____, he will make us stay after school.

11 **Match the sentences. Write the letters.**

_b_ **1** My friend lends me a video game.   **a** He gets upset.

___ **2** I don't do my chores.   **b** I take really good care of the disk.

___ **3** A classmate cheats on a test.   **c** The teacher calls the parents.

___ **4** I tell my friend that I lied to him.   **d** I apologize to my parents.

12 **Write sentences using the ideas in 11.**

1 If my friend lends me a video game, I'll take really good care of the disk.

2 _____

3 _____

4 _____

How did I do? ☆☆☆☆☆

> You **should tell** your parents **if** you have a problem at school. **If** you don't want to get in trouble, you **shouldn't lie**.

13 **Complete the advice column with the correct form of the verbs in the box. Add should if necessary.**

| call | find | give | say | start | stop | tell | tell |

Ask Jenna and Jack: Smart Advice for Kids

Dear Jenna,
My friend keeps calling me names like "stupid" and "idiot." She always apologizes later, but it makes me upset. I told her to stop, but she doesn't. What should I do?

Sad Samantha

Dear Sad Samantha,
This girl is NOT your friend! If this girl **1**_____ you names again, you **2**_____ her to apologize immediately. If she **3**_____ *no*, you **4**_____ a new friend!

Jenna

Dear Jack,
My little brother is always following me around. I feel guilty when I tell him to stop, because he cries, but I don't want him hanging around. My friends don't like it either. What should I do?

Guilty Gordon

Dear Guilty Gordon,
This is a difficult problem. Arrange times to play with your little brother. Then tell him that he can't follow you with your friends. If he **5**_____ to follow you and your friends, you **6**_____ him to stop. Say that you and he will play together later. If he **7**_____ following you, you **8**_____ him a reward. Good luck!

Jack

14 **Complete the sentences with advice. Use should or shouldn't.**

1 If you borrow something from a friend, _____.

2 If someone is mean to you, _____.

3 If you have a problem at school, _____.

How did I do? ☆☆☆☆☆

45

15 **Listen and read. What does "character" mean?**

Ethics
1 **Ethics** is knowing what good and bad behavior is. You make choices based on ethics about what's **morally** right or wrong, or what's fair or unfair.
2 Your **character** is all of your **traits** and qualities taken together, such as being friendly, honest, and hard-working.
3 **Treat** means how you act towards others. Do you **treat** people nicely or are you mean?
4 **Ethical behavior** is when you do the right thing and treat someone fairly and respectfully. Ethical behavior is good and fair behavior, which is acceptable in a given situation.
5 It is important to try to see things from the right **perspective**, so that we understand things well and make good decisions.
6 You should always try to behave in an **acceptable** way, so that you don't upset or harm yourself or others.

16 **Unscramble and write. Then make up a sentence with each word.**

1 _____ srecepftlu

_____

2 _____ hetcial

_____

3 _____ rpepscevtie

_____

4 _____ roamlyl

_____

5 _____ cacpetleab

_____

6 _____ ratet

_____

How did I do? ☆ ☆ ☆ ☆ ☆

17 **Match the proverbs with their meanings. Write the letters.**

___ **1** "A clear conscience (mind) is a soft pillow."

a I don't need friends if they aren't good friends.

___ **2** "Better to be alone than to be in bad company."

b I trust my friends to tell me the truth about myself.

___ **3** "A friend's eye is a good mirror."

c If I don't tell the truth, I won't be able to sleep at night.

47

18 **Listen and read. Match the stories with the proverbs above. Write 1, 2, or 3.**

Problems and Proverbs

All around the world, in every culture, people use proverbs to explain things about life or human nature. Proverbs are short sayings that give advice and help us to make decisions. Some proverbs tell us about ourselves and our friends, as in the three stories below about friendships.

Dilemma A: ___
Nellie is a new girl at school. She's very shy so she finds it hard to make friends. A group of girls asks Nellie if she wants to be friends with them. Nellie is very happy to say yes. She feels like she's part of a group and is happy because the girls are fun to be with. But Nellie begins to notice that these girls are loud in class and don't pay much attention to the teacher. The girls notice that Nellie is good at math. They ask her to do their math homework. They say that if she doesn't, they'll tell lies about her. Nellie feels very hurt. She tells the girls that she won't be their friend anymore. The girls tell lies about Nellie, but Nellie doesn't care. She walks alone to school and feels good about herself.

Dilemma B: ___
Doug hasn't been doing his homework. He's stopped hanging out with his friends. He just wants to make robots and listen to music. He keeps making promises to people, but he never keeps them. Today, he was supposed to help Calvin fix his bike, but he didn't. Calvin stops by Doug's house. He says that Doug isn't acting like a friend. He's not being responsible. Calvin tells Doug that he should talk to his parents or to a teacher at school. Doug gets really angry and says that Calvin is stupid. Calvin leaves. Doug thinks about his behavior and realizes that Calvin is probably right. Calvin's a good friend.

Dilemma C: ___
Gloria and Zoe are Tina's best friends. They tell Tina that they stole some bracelets at the craft fair at school last Saturday. Tina's teacher thinks she saw Donna near the bracelets so now everyone thinks that Donna took them. Tina doesn't know Donna well, but she feels awful. Gloria and Zoe beg Tina not to tell anyone. They say they won't do it again. Tina feels very guilty. She decides to tell the truth anyway. She feels good about the decision, but very sad about her friends. She hopes they understand and that they can stay friends. She knows they just made a stupid mistake.

How did I do? ☆☆☆☆☆

A well-written story ends in a way that seems "right" or possible for the main character. Here are ways to help you decide what endings are "right" or possible:

• Find information in the story about the character's traits.

• Notice how the character treats others.

• Look at the character's actions and feelings.

19 **Look at 5. Circle the traits that describe Gary's character in "Gary's Dilemma".**

| caring | funny | honest | lazy | mean | not honest | serious | worried |

20 **Complete the sentences about Gary. Include one of the traits you circled in 19 and ideas from the story. Use the ideas in the box or your own ideas.**

| asks his parents what he should do | says nothing and hopes that Ryan is OK |
| tells a teacher about Ryan | tells Ryan's parents |

I think that Gary is _____ (trait) because in the story he _____

_____.

It's possible that he'll _____.

I don't think that Gary will _____.

21 **Think about Gary's character. What does he do the next day? Think about these questions.**

What is the first thing that he does? What happens to Gary and Ryan? Are they still friends? Why/Why not?

22 **Write an ending to "Gary's Dilemma" in your notebook. Look at 19, 20, and 21 to help you.**

The next day, Gary made a decision. He should...

How did I do? ☆ ☆ ☆ ☆ ☆

Review

23 **Match the expressions with the situations. Write the letters.**

___ **1** tell the truth

___ **2** feel guilty

___ **3** cheat

___ **4** feel good

___ **5** get into trouble

___ **6** be upset with

a Amy looked at Suzie's test and copied the answers.

b Steve's mom is angry with him because he didn't do his homework.

c Meg feels bad because she hurt Evan's feelings.

d Mike hit Ryan on the playground and he had to go to the principal's office.

e Jeff said that Claire took the money. She did.

f Monica helped Robert study for his test. She's happy she could help him.

24 **Write what will happen. Use will and the words in parentheses.**

1 Maya knows her brother cheated on a test. She wants to <u>tell her parents</u>. What will her brother do? (be / upset)

<u>If Maya tells her parents, her brother will be very upset with her.</u>

2 Janet stole some money from her mom. She wants to <u>apologize to her mom</u>. What will her mom do? (say / disappointed)

_____

3 Ivy got into trouble because she was with a group of girls who called a young boy names and made him cry. She wants to <u>apologize</u>. What will he probably do? (say / OK)

_____

How did I do? ☆ ☆ ☆ ☆ ☆

1 **Unscramble the words. Complete the phrases.**

School Activities

1 hand in an _____
2 do a _____
3 study for a _____
4 do _____
5 finish a science _____

ttse _____

_____ oobk oerprt

hmwokroe _____

_____ sseamgnint

rojctep _____

_____ ylap

pbishlu _____

_____ cblmi

boemec _____

_____ teme

Reaching Goals

1 _____ a book
2 _____ a doctor
3 _____ an instrument
4 _____ a world leader
5 _____ a mountain

Making Choices

1 _____ in a test
2 _____ guilty
3 be _____
4 _____ the truth
5 get into _____

tspeu _____

_____ toruble

fele _____

_____ eltl

cetah _____

2 **Find a song that makes you think about school days, goals, or dilemmas. Complete the chart.**

Song Title _____

Singer's or group's name: _____

What language is used in the song? _____

How long have you liked this singer/group? _____

How long has this singer/group been performing? _____

What's the song about? _____

What happens in the song? _____

_____

If you could change words (lyrics) in the song, which lyrics would you change?

_____

_____

3 **Draw pictures to illustrate your song. Then write the story of your song on a separate piece of paper.**

Dreams for the Future

Language in Context

1 **Match the pictures with the predictions. Write the numbers. Then ✓ when you think the predictions may come true.**

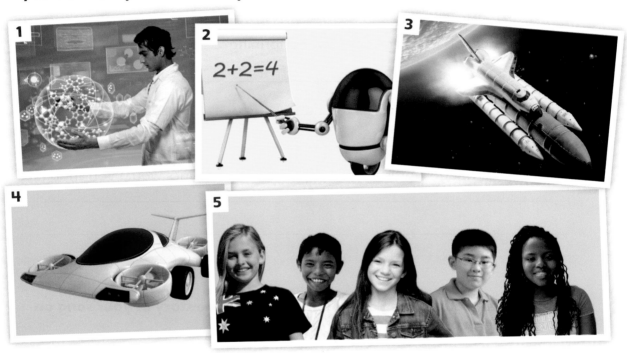

Predictions for the Future	Now	In My Lifetime	Never
___ **a** Spaceships to other planets will be departing daily.			
___ **b** Robots will be teaching in the classroom.			
___ **c** People around the world will be living happily together.			
___ **d** We'll be driving flying cars.			
___ **e** We'll be making progress towards finding cures for many serious diseases.			

2 **Look at 1. Explain one of your predictions.**

_____

_____

3   **Match the pictures with the phrases.**

In the future, I'll be...

running my own business

raising a family

living in another country

working in my dream job

earning a good salary

4   **Complete the sentences with the phrases in 3.**

1   In 20 years, I'll be _____. I really want children!

2   In 10 years, I'll be _____. I'll be a cartoonist. I've always wanted to draw cartoons. It'll be perfect!

3   In 10 years, I'll be _____ and I won't worry about money.

4   In 20 years, I'll be _____. I won't work for anyone. I'll be the boss!

5   In 10 years, I'll be _____. I'm not sure where. Maybe in France.

5   **Unscramble the sentences. Are they true or false for you? Circle T for true or F for false.**

1   be / my / won't / I / running / own business
   In 20 years, _____.   **T**   **F**

2   a family / won't / I / raising / be /
   In 10 years, _____.   **T**   **F**

THINK BIG

Do you think the world will be a better or worse place 30 years from now? Why?

How did I do? ☆☆☆☆☆

55

6 **Listen and read the email. Then ✓ the predictions Christina makes about her classmates.**

TO	
CC	
SUBJECT	Christina's Predictions

Dear sixth grade students,

As class blogger, it's my job to write about our experiences as sixth grade students. I've been thinking a lot about my future lately and, since you know how curious and nosey I am, I can't help but think about your futures, too. It's never too early to think about what we'll be doing 10 or 20 years from now. I thought it'd be fun to start the conversation. This is what I predict:

I'll start with me. I know that in 10 years, I'll be running my own business in the fashion industry. That doesn't surprise you, does it? You know how I love fashion and I also love being the boss! One thing I won't be doing is living in this city! I want to live abroad – maybe in Tokyo or Paris. Now, what about Jessie? I think he'll be working in his dream job as a cartoonist because that's all I see him doing at school. I bet he'll be making animated films. In 10 years, Stephanie will definitely be working in the music industry. She has an amazing voice. Don't you agree? George will be taking adventurous trips abroad because he'll be a famous journalist. He's very smart and he works so hard. I hope that all of my predictions come true!

That's not all, but that's all I have time for now. If you want to reply, let me know your dreams and I'll add them to the school blog. Let's all think about our dreams and reach for the stars this year!

Your class blogger,

Christina

Predictions

1 working in his dream job

2 living in this city

3 working in the music industry

4 speaking foreign languages

5 earning a good salary

6 married

7 famous

8 taking adventurous trips

7 **Make a prediction about what you'll be doing in 20 years and explain why.**

I'll be _____ because _____.

How did I do? ☆ ☆ ☆ ☆ ☆

Language in Action

8 Listen and read. Then circle the correct answers.

Brandon: What do you think you'll be doing after you graduate from high school, Serena?

Serena: College, I'm sure. How about you? What will you be doing in, say, 15 years?

Brandon: I'll be working on a big movie!

Serena: A movie? You think you'll be a movie star after you graduate?

Brandon: No, not a movie star. A movie director. I'll be working with all the big Hollywood stars.

Serena: Really? And how will you do that?

Brandon: Well, I'm pretty good at making short movies on my computer right now. I just need one big break, and *voilà*! I'll be the next Spielberg!

Serena: Sure. I just hope you won't forget us once you're rich and famous!

Brandon: Of course not! Mom and you will be walking on the red carpet with me!

Serena: Oh, I like that idea!

1 What does Brandon think he'll be doing in 15 years?

    a He'll be acting in movies.   **b** He'll be directing movies.
    c He'll be in college.

2 Young actors and singers are always looking for a big break in their career. What does *a big break* mean?

    a a big rest   **b** a chance to be successful
    c a chance to travel

3 When an actor is *on the red carpet*, what is he or she invited to attend?

    a an important event   **b** college
    c a reading of the movie script

4 The word *voilá* is French. People say "voilá" when they show or tell you the result. What is the result of Brandon's big break?

    a He'll meet Steven Spielberg.   **b** He'll be a famous director like Steven Spielberg.
    c He'll be speaking French to everyone.

9 Read the dialog in 8 again. Does Brandon think he'll be successful? Why/Why not?

_____

_____

_____

How did I do? ☆☆☆☆☆

Grammar

What **will** you **be doing** ten years from now?

I'**ll** <u>definitely</u> **be studying** at a big university.

Where **will** you **be living** in twenty years?

I <u>probably</u> **won't be living** in Europe.

10 Match. Then answer the questions. Use the future progressive form of the verbs and definitely or probably.

Hopes and Dreams in 20 years

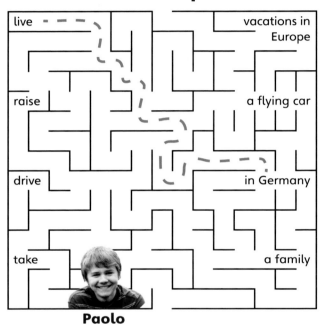

live
vacations in Europe
raise
a flying car
drive
in Germany
take
a family

Paolo

live
a good salary
speak
several foreign languages
work
in a big city
earn
in my dream job

Carine

1 Where will you be living in 20 years?

Paolo: <u>I'll probably be living in Germany.</u> _____ (probably)

2 What will you be driving in 20 years?

Paolo: _____ (definitely)

3 Where will you be taking vacations in 20 years?

Paolo: _____ (probably)

4 Where will you be living in 20 years?

Carine: _____ (definitely)

5 What will you be doing in 20 years?

Carine: _____ (probably)

How did I do? ☆ ☆ ☆ ☆ ☆

Will you **be running** a business?	No, <u>definitely</u> not./I <u>definitely</u> **won't**… Yes, <u>definitely</u>./I'**ll** <u>definitely</u>… <u>Probably</u> not./I <u>probably</u> **won't**… Yes, <u>probably</u>./I'**ll** <u>probably</u>…

11   **Answer the questions. Use the information in** 10**.**

1   Will Carine be working in her dream job in 20 years?

_____

2   Will Paolo be living in Germany in 20 years?

_____

3   Will Paolo be taking vacations in Asia?

_____

4   Will Carine be earning a good salary in 20 years?

_____

12   **Answer the questions about your future life in college. Use** probably **or** definitely**.**

1   Will you be seeing your family a lot when you go to college?

_____

2   Will you be studying a foreign language in college?

_____

3   Will you be studying harder than you do now?

_____

13   **Choose a friend. Write a question about your friend's future life in college. Ask your friend the question and write their answer.**

Q: _____

A: _____

How did I do? ☆ ☆ ☆ ☆ ☆

60

14 **Read and complete with the words in the box. Then listen and check.**

| imagine | nanotechnology | 3-D | virtual | wireless |

Two Trends in Medicine

Futurists, whose job is to study the future and help people to prepare for the future, are talking about two important trends in the future of medicine. A trend is the way something is developing or changing, and these two trends in medicine may revolutionize the way illnesses and diseases are diagnosed and treated by doctors in the future.

One important trend in the future of medicine is ¹_____. The word nano means billionth. That's really tiny! Scientists who are working in nanotechnology are studying particles that are so small that they are invisible to the human eye! In fact, they have to measure these particles with a new unit of measurement, called the nanometer. Do you see the word "meter" in nanometer? You know how long a meter is, don't you?

Can you ²_____ something that is only 1/1,000,000,000 of a baseball bat? One example of this is the nanobot. These microscopic robots are made of the same material that we are made of: DNA. In the future, scientists will be using nanobots to treat diseases and illnesses. For example, when you become ill in the future, doctors will put a nanobot into your body. The robot will find the cause of your illness and give you the correct medicine to help it heal.

The second trend in the future is in ³_____ medicine. Thirty years from now, when you have a fever and feel ill, you won't have to leave the house and go to a doctor. You'll be using ⁴_____ technology to diagnose and treat your illness in your own home. In this futuristic scenario, you'll take ⁵_____ pictures of your body using an object like a TV remote control. You'll upload these images to a website. The doctor will download the images, review them, and upload medicine for you to download. If the doctor wants to talk to you, he or she will talk to you through a video call – or maybe he or she will "visit" you using 3-D technology. The doctor will look like he or she is in your house but it will just be a 3-D image. Wouldn't that be amazing?

15 **Read 14 again and circle the correct answers.**

1 The word *nano* means a ___.

  a millionth   **b** billionth

2 In the future, a doctor will look at 3-D ___ of your body in order to treat you.

  a objects   **b** images

3 Virtual medicine makes use of wireless ___ in your home.

  a technology   **b** pictures

How did I do? ☆☆☆☆☆

16 **Read and complete. Then listen and check.**

62

| hydroelectric | solar | electricity | energy | Geothermal |

Renewable energy

As the number of people in the world increases, the demand for energy increases.

To meet this demand, many countries are turning to renewable energy.

In Iceland, there are lots of active volcanoes which produce heat.

¹_____ energy plants turn this heat into ²_____

and heating power.

In South America, they use water to produce electricity. The Itaipu Dam is a powerful

³_____ dam.

In Morocco, they are building a large ⁴_____ power plant which will use

the powerful desert sun to get ⁵_____.

17 **How will renewable energy help you live in the future?**

I will cook on a solar stove.

I will heat my house with geothermal energy.

_____

_____

_____

_____

How did I do? ☆☆☆☆☆

When you write an email, you need to think about who you're writing to. If you're writing to a teacher or other adult, you'll write a formal email. If you're writing to a friend, you'll write an informal email. Here are some ways these two kinds of emails are different.

	Formal email	Informal email
1 Subject	1 Be clear and specific. *This week's essay*	1 Write something simple. *Tonight* or *Hi*
2 Greeting	2 Use Ms. / Mr. / Mrs. *Mrs. Smith,*	2 Write *Hi, Tony* or *Hey, Tony,*
3 Body	3 Write your message in full sentences, check your spelling, and be polite. *I missed school yesterday because I was ill. Can you tell me what the homework is, please?*	3 u can use short words coz u wanna write quickly to ur bff.
4 Closing	4 Write *Yours sincerely,* or *Best wishes,* and your name below.	4 Write your name.

18 **Read each sentence. Write formal if it belongs in a formal email or informal if it belongs in an informal email.**

1 _____ Hey, Tami,

2 _____ I am having trouble deciding what to do for my science project. Could you help me think of some ideas?

3 _____ c u later bff!

4 _____ Dear Mr. Taylor,

5 _____ Yours sincerely, Steve

6 _____ Wanna play video games at my house?

19 **Look at 18. Write a formal email to Mr. Taylor and an informal email to Tami in your notebook. In the informal email, use abbreviations from the box.**

TIPS

Texting Abbreviations

b4 = before
bff = best friends forever
c = see
coz = because
gonna = going to
TTYL = talk to you later
u = you
wanna = want to

How did I do? ☆☆☆☆☆

Review

20   **Complete the text. Use the future progressive of the verbs in parentheses.**

Carlos and his sister Bianca have big plans for the future. Carlos [1]_____
probably _____ (go) to college in ten years. Once he graduates,
he [2]_____ (work) as a businessman with his dad. He definitely
[3]_____ (not live) in another country because he wants to
stay close to his family in Mexico City.

Bianca [4]_____ probably _____ (start) her
studies in chemistry. She has always wanted to be a scientist. In 20
years, she [5]_____ definitely _____ (earn)
a good salary. She probably [6]_____ (not live) in Mexico
because she has always wanted to live in a foreign country.

Both Carlos and Bianca [7]_____ (raise) big families. They both want
to have lots of children.

21   **Choose a family member. Complete the sentences about his/her future using the future progressive. Use will or won't and the words from the box or your own words.**

	dream job earning a good salary famous		
married running his or her own business taking adventurous vacations			

1   My family member's name is _____.

2   This person _____ in 10 years.

3   This person _____ in 20 years.

22   **Answer the questions. Use Yes, definitely, Yes, probably, No, probably not, or No, definitely not.**

1   In your lifetime, do you think you will be working with intelligent beings from outer space?

_____

2   Do you think people will be living on other planets in the next century?

_____

How did I do? ☆ ☆ ☆ ☆ ☆

5 If I Could Fly...

Language in Context

1 Which super powers do these characters have? Match the characters with their super power. Write the numbers.

___ **a** able to climb tall buildings

___ **b** has superhuman strength

___ **c** runs at lightning speed

___ **d** becomes invisible with the snap of a finger

___ **e** saves the world from bad guys

___ **f** travels through time and space

2 Look at **1** and answer the questions.

1 Which super power would make your life better?

_____

2 How would the super power improve your life?

_____

3 Who are your favorite superheroes? What powers do they have?

_____

3 **Match the beginning of the phrases with their endings. Then label the pictures.**

___ **1** run at

___ **2** travel

___ **3** have

___ **4** become

a invisible

b superhuman strength

c lightning speed

d through time

A _____ B _____ C _____ D _____

4 **Complete the sentences with the phrases in 3.**

1 I want to meet people who lived long ago. If I could have a super power,
I would _____.

2 I want to move around without people being able to see me. If I could have a super
power, I would _____.

3 I want to be able to get anywhere in a few seconds! If I could have a super power,
I would _____.

4 I want to be really strong so that I can pick up anything I want! If I could
have a super power, I would _____.

5 **Complete the sentences. If you had these super powers, what would you do?**

1 If I could have superhuman strength, I would _____.

2 If I could read minds, I would _____.

3 If I could travel through time, I would _____.

THINK BIG

Which super powers could help the police? How?

_____

_____

How did I do? ☆☆☆☆☆

6 **Listen and read. Then circle T for true or F for false.** 69

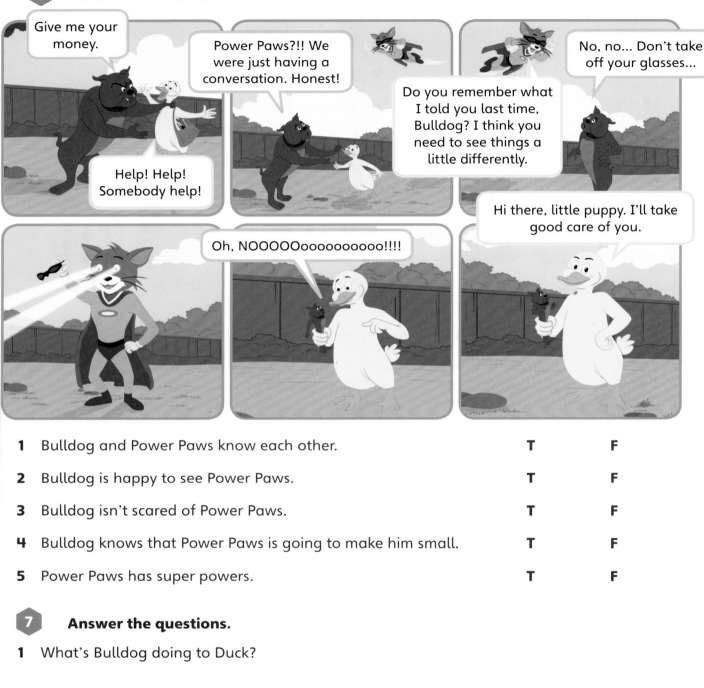

		T	F
1	Bulldog and Power Paws know each other.	T	F
2	Bulldog is happy to see Power Paws.	T	F
3	Bulldog isn't scared of Power Paws.	T	F
4	Bulldog knows that Power Paws is going to make him small.	T	F
5	Power Paws has super powers.	T	F

7 **Answer the questions.**

1 What's Bulldog doing to Duck?

_____

2 Why is Power Paws going to make Bulldog small?

_____

3 Do you think Duck will take good care of Bulldog?

_____

How did I do? ☆ ☆ ☆ ☆ ☆

Language in Action

8 **Listen and read. Then circle the correct answers.**

Girl: Dad, do you think we'll ever be able to travel through time?

Dad: Wow, <u>that's a hard one</u>. A lot's possible today, but I really don't see how time travel would be. Why do you ask?

Girl: I was just wondering. Imagine how much fun it would be if we could! If you could <u>go back in time</u>, where would you go?

Dad: Hmm. <u>Let me think</u>... Maybe I'd go back to see my great-grandparents who lived in London. My great-grandfather was a shoemaker there – have I ever told you that? I'm told he was <u>quite a character</u>. I'd love to talk to him. What would you do?

Girl: Me? Oh, I already know – that's easy. If I could travel through time, I'd go back to last night and review more. I don't feel ready for my math test this afternoon!

1 The girl's dad thinks the girl's question is ___ to answer.

   a easy   **b** not easy

2 The girl ___ travel back in time.

   a wants to   **b** doesn't want to

3 The girl's dad ___ stories about his great-grandfather.

   a has heard   **b** hasn't heard

4 The girl ___ hard for her math test.

   a studied   **b** didn't study

9 **Look at 8. Read the underlined expressions. Match the expressions with their meanings. Write the letters.**

___ **1** That's a hard one.   **a** It means "to travel to a time in the past."

___ **2** go back in time   **b** It means "a funny, interesting, unique person" that people like.

___ **3** quite a character   **c** It means "I need a little time to think about my answer."

___ **4** Let me think.   **d** It means "That's a difficult question." You say this when the question isn't easy to answer.

10 **Complete the sentence. Use a phrase from 9.**

The teacher asks you, "Who's your favorite superhero?" You need to think about your answer so you say _____.

How did I do? ☆ ☆ ☆ ☆ ☆

Grammar

if clause	result clause
If I **were** you,	I**'d choose** something else.
If he **made** his bed every day,	his mom **would be** happy.
If she **could have** one superpower,	she**'d become** invisible.

11 **Complete the sentences with the words given.**

1 (would, study, were) If I _____ you,
I _____ harder. You would get better grades.

2 (could, would, fly, visit) If she _____,
she _____ her aunt and uncle in California all the time.

3 (could, would, run, win) If the track team _____ at lightning
speed, they _____ all their tournaments.

4 (would, be, did) If all the students _____ their homework all the
time, the teacher _____ happy.

12 **Read. Complete the sentences with the words in parentheses and could and would.**

I can't sing well. But if I _____
(sing) well, I _____ (join) a band.

My friends and I can't travel back in time. If
we _____ (travel) back in
time, we _____ (meet) our
favorite heroes in history.

My older brother can't drive yet. If he
_____ (drive), he
_____ (take) my friends
and me to the movies.

My friend can't be quiet in class. If she
_____ (be) quiet, our
teacher _____ (be) happier.

13 **Complete the sentences about yourself.**

1 If I could meet a famous person, I _____.

2 _____, I would be very happy.

How did I do?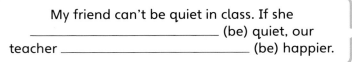

> If you **didn't have to go** to school, what **would** you **do** every day?
>
> If I **didn't have to go** to school, I **would stay** home and **listen** to music all day.
>
> If you **could go** anywhere, where **would** you **go**?
>
> If I **could go** anywhere, I'**d go** to Paris.

14 **Unscramble the questions.**

1 (you / would / go / where)

If you could visit any country you wanted to, _____?

2 (would / which language / you / study)

If you could study another language _____?

3 (you / be / would / which animal)

If you could be any animal, _____?

4 (be / who / you / would)

If you could be any superhero, _____?

5 (would / play / what / you)

If you could play any instrument, _____?

15 **Match the questions in 14 with the answers below. Write the numbers. Then circle T for true or F for false.**

___ **1** I would be a wolf because wolves are really smart animals.   T   F

___ **2** I would visit Italy to see the art.   T   F

___ **3** I would study Chinese.   T   F

___ **4** I would be Spider-Man because I think it would be fun to climb walls.   T   F

___ **5** I would play the piano.   T   F

16 **Ask three questions in 14 to a friend or family member. Write his or her answers.**

1 _____

2 _____

3 _____

How did I do? ☆ ☆ ☆ ☆ ☆

74

17 Listen and read. Match the titles A–E with the paragraphs 1–5.

A Super sticky adhesive

B Perfect memory

C What do you think?

D Inventive products

E Super computers

Super Power or Invention?

1 ☐ Some researchers have developed products that seem to give us super power-like abilities. One of these inventions is the super sticky adhesive that they created by studying geckos and their sticky feet. Another invention would allow us to use our minds to tell a computer what to do. A third invention is our ability to visualize a computer anywhere we want one – even on our hands. Let's imagine what our lives might be like if we could buy these products today.

2 ☐ In the morning, you wake up. Your bed is stuck on the wall so you climb down a ladder to get to the floor. There is space under your bed now to hang out with friends so you like that. After breakfast, you put on your super sticky shoes and hand pads. On your way to school, you activate them and you climb up a wall to your friend Timmy's bedroom window. He sees you. You both climb down the wall and start walking to school.

3 ☐ "Oh, no!" you suddenly say, "I forgot my homework!" You think, "Mom, please send my math homework to school." Your mom gets the message on her smartphone and texts back, "OK." You think, "Thanks, Mom!" Your mind is connected to your computer at home so you can send messages to it or to your parents' smartphones. Then your friend says, "I wonder what the reviews are for the new superhero movie?" He draws a box on your backpack and a computer appears. He goes to a movie review website and reads the latest reviews to you as you walk.

4 ☐ At school, you climb up the wall and hang your jacket on a hook. Your teacher gives you a quiz and tells you, "Don't draw computers anywhere. If you've studied, you'll know every answer." You didn't study much so you're thinking, "If I could see the book in my mind, I could look up the answers." Researchers haven't worked out how to give you perfect memory – but they're probably working on it.

5 ☐ Thus, if we had these three inventions today, the possibilities would be endless. Think of all the things you could do with super sticky adhesive. Also, what would you tell a computer to do with your mind? Think of the many uses this super power would have for you. Imagine being able to visualize a computer whenever you need one, too. Life with these inventions would be very different from now. You would be a real superhero! What do you think?

18 Read 17 again and circle T for true or F for false.

1 Researchers created super sticky adhesive from studying geckos' tongues.   T   F

2 One invention is the ability to control a computer with our minds.   T   F

3 You could stick your bed to the wall with super sticky adhesive.   T   F

4 A third invention is the super power ability to remember things perfectly.   T   F

5 If we had these inventions, life would be very different for us today.   T   F

How did I do? ☆☆☆☆☆

19 **Listen and read. Write the names of the superheroes.**

Superhuman Superheroes!

Superheroes from around the world have unique abilities to help them protect people and destroy evil. Many superheroes have suffered a trauma and want to save people from the same thing that happened to them. Other superheroes got their super powers from something that happened to them accidentally. Many superheroes originated in the U.S.A., but some countries have their own superheroes. Here are some examples:

Cat Girl Nuku Nuku is a native of Japan. She's a college student but when something terrible happens, she becomes a superhero! She can react quickly, just like a cat. She can smell, see, and hear very well because she has the senses of a cat. She also has superhuman strength.

Meteorix is from Mexico. He's at college, too, and his everyday name is Aldo. He also has superhuman strength and can throw bolts of lightning. When he has to protect himself, he covers himself with blue armor by swallowing a meteorite.

Darna is a native of the Philippines. Her everyday name is Narda and she's a student as well. Darna can fly and has superhuman strength and speed. She can't be destroyed by weapons that humans make. She can change back and forth between her two identities, Darna and Narda, by swallowing a stone and shouting the name of her other identity.

Superheroes are fun to read about, but do you sometimes wish that they were real? If these superheroes were real, they would have a lot to do every day!

1   Human weapons cannot destroy this superhero. _____

2   Bolts of lightning are weapons of this superhero. _____

3   This superhero acts like a cat. _____

20   **Unscramble and write words from 19. Then complete the sentences.**

1   _____   liev   Many superheroes help to destroy _____.

2   _____   nseess   Cat Girl has the _____ of a cat.

3   _____   lbost   Meteroix can throw _____ of lightning.

4   _____   awenosp   Darna can't be destroyed by human _____.

How did I do? ☆☆☆☆☆

When you write a description of a character, describe everything about that character:

1	name(s)	**2**	appearance
3	occupation	**4**	super powers
5	country of origin	**6**	family
7	time period that he or she lives in: now, the future, the past	**8**	mission

21 **Read the sentences and match them with the information in the box. What information is missing? Write the numbers.**

____ Her everyday name is Diana, but her superhero name is Wonder Woman.

____ She has superhuman strength and she's an excellent fighter. She has a rope that makes people tell the truth and an invisible jet.

____ She comes from a place near ancient Greece.

____ She has a lot of sisters.

Missing information: Numbers ____ ____ ____ ____

22 **Read the missing information from 21 below. Number it according to the information in the writing box.**

____ She lived in the past and lives in the present, too.	____ She makes villains honest.
____ In many stories she's an officer in the army.	____ She is tall / has long dark hair.

23 **Write a description of Wonder Woman. Use the information in 21 and 22.**

_____

_____

_____

_____

_____

How did I do? ☆ ☆ ☆ ☆ ☆

24 **Read and match. Write the letters.**

___ **1** If I could read people's minds,

___ **2** If I could run at lightning speed,

___ **3** If I could travel through time,

___ **4** If I could fly,

a I'd be faster than a jet plane.

b I'd know what they were thinking.

c I'd go back and play with my grandpa when he was young.

d I'd take my sisters and brothers for rides in the sky with me.

25 **Complete the sentences with your own ideas.**

1 If _____, I'd know why you are upset with me.

2 If _____, I'd move your house closer to mine. Then I could see you more often.

3 If I could invent something to help other people, _____.

4 If I _____, my family would be very happy.

26 **Read. Circle the correct answers.**

1 If people ___ wings, they wouldn't drive cars.

   a have   **b** had

2 If she had enough money, she ___ those earrings. But she doesn't have enough money.

   a 'd buy   **b** buys

3 You're really smart. If I ___ you, I'd try out for a TV game show.

   a were   **b** be

4 If my older brother went to bed earlier, he ___ so tired every morning.

   a is not going to be   **b** would not be

27 **Answer the questions with your own ideas.**

1 If you found 20 dollars, what would you do with the money?

2 If you wrote a book, what would you write about?

3 If you owned a flying car, where would you go and why?

How did I do? ☆☆☆☆☆

6 The Coolest School Subjects

Language in Context

1 **Match the pictures with the school subjects. Write the numbers.**

1

2

3

4

5

6

___ **a** geography

___ **b** music

___ **c** art history

___ **d** world history

___ **e** science

___ **f** P.E.

2 **If you could choose three subjects to add to your school schedule, what would they be? ✓ or add your own ideas.**

- ☐ computer science
- ☐ Chinese
- ☐ orchestra
- ☐ theater
- ☐ _____

- ☐ government
- ☐ chemistry
- ☐ tennis
- ☐ ecosystems and ecology
- ☐ _____

3 Unscramble the words. Use the words to complete the sentences.

1 M Y C R O E A C D _____

The word _____ comes from a Greek word that means "power of the people". One of the first western examples of this form of government was in Athens, in the fifth century BC.

2 M A M L A M _____

The cheetah is the fastest _____ in the world. It can run about 100 meters in six seconds!

3 P T N A L _____

The bladderwort is the deadliest meat-eating _____. It can kill an insect in less than a millisecond.

4 G I Y R H W A L T P S _____

Shakespeare is one of the most famous _____ in English literature. He wrote approximately 40 plays in his lifetime, including comedies, tragedies, and historical plays.

5 P E R M I   B E U R N M _____ _____

The number 8 can be divided by 1 and 8, but it can also be divided by 2 and 4. As a result, it is not a _____ _____.

4 Match the sentences with the subjects. Write the letters.

___ **1** I want to learn more about myths and legends.

___ **2** I love reading about democracies all over the world.

___ **3** We have a grammar test today.

___ **4** I love playing soccer!

___ **5** We're painting a mural on the wall today.

___ **6** In today's lesson, we learned that blue whales are the largest mammals in the world!

a P.E.

b English

c literature

d art

e social studies

f science (biology)

THINK BIG

Is what you learn inside the classroom and what you learn outside the classroom equally important? Why/Why not?

_____

_____

How did I do? ☆ ☆ ☆ ☆ ☆

83

5 **Listen and read. Then answer the questions.**

The Story of Daedalus and Icarus

Once upon a time, on the island of Crete, there was a man named Daedalus and his young son Icarus. They lived in the palace of King Minos. Daedalus was the smartest man in the palace. He was also one of the greatest inventors and architects of that time. He invented many things for the king, including an enormous type of maze called The Labyrinth. King Minos didn't want Daedalus to share the secrets of The Labyrinth with anyone so he put Daedalus and Icarus in prison. Daedalus was very unhappy. He had only one wish. He wanted to be free.

One day, Daedalus was watching the birds fly. He admired their beautiful, strong wings. Watching the birds gave him an idea. If he created wings for Icarus and himself, they could fly away and be free! So Daedalus created wings of feathers and wax and they put them on. Daedalus told Icarus, "Be careful! Don't fly too close to the water or you might fall into it! Don't fly too close to the sun or the wax will melt and you'll fall!" Icarus said that he would obey his father, but when they started flying, Icarus became extremely excited. He flew in circles and went higher and higher. He loved the feeling of freedom and flying. His father called out to him, "Come back here! Don't go too close to the sun!" Icarus wanted to listen, but the feeling of freedom was the best feeling in the world so he kept flying higher. The sun became hotter and hotter, and began to melt the wax. Icarus started to fly lower, but it was too late. Icarus's wings fell off and he fell into the sea and was lost.

1 Why did King Minos put Daedalus and Icarus in prison?

_____

2 Why did Daedalus want to escape?

_____

3 Why did Icarus fly higher and higher?

_____

4 What can we learn from this story?

_____

5 The Icarian Sea was named after Icarus. Do you know any other places named after famous myths and legends? Write the names.

_____

How did I do? ☆☆☆☆☆

86
6 Listen and read. Then circle the correct answers.

379009

Julie: I haven't reviewed for the math test yet, have you?

Leo: Not yet. Hey, <u>let's make a study group</u>!

Julie: That's the smartest idea you've had in a long time!

Leo: Ha! Ha! Very funny.

Cathy: Great idea! The only thing I remember about prime numbers is that they're larger than 1.

Julie: <u>Speaking of</u> prime numbers, do you know the most amazing thing about the numbers 3-7-9-0-0-9? Type them on a calculator and read them upside down. They spell *GOOGLE*.

Leo: <u>Seriously</u>? <u>Let me see</u>… You're right! That's the coolest thing ever!

1 Why are Julie, Leo, and Cathy going to get together?

    a They're going to have fun.   **b** They're going to review for the math test.

2 Why is 379009 an amazing number?

    a It spells the word *GOOGLE* in numbers.   **b** It's the largest prime number.

7 Look at 6. Read the underlined expressions. Match the expressions with their meanings. Write the letters.

____**1** Let's make a study group

____**2** Speaking of…

____**3** Seriously?

____**4** Let me see.

    a By the way, that reminds me of something.

    b Really? I'm surprised.

    c Why don't we study together?

    d I want to try.

87
8 Complete the dialog with the expressions in 7. Then listen and check.

A: I was just chosen to be on a TV quiz program.

B: ¹_____? Congratulations!

01134

A: Yeah, they asked me what happens when you turn 01134 upside down. I said it spells *hello*.

B: ²_____. Wow! You're right!

A: ³_____ numbers, ⁴_____ for the math test tomorrow.

B: Good idea!

How did I do? ☆☆☆☆☆

Grammar

China has **more** speakers of English **than** the U.S.A.
I have **fewer** school subjects **than** my brother.
Teachers in Finland give **less** homework **than** teachers in the U.K. do.

9 **Circle the correct words to complete these facts about countries.**

1 People in Germany spend 18 hours a week watching TV. People in the U.S.A. spend 21 hours. People in Germany spend **less** / **more** time watching TV than people in the U.S.A.

2 According to the World Atlas, Europe has 47 countries and Asia has 44 countries. There are **more** / **less** countries in Europe than in Asia.

3 In Mexico, there are approximately 55 million men and 57 million women. There are **less** / **fewer** men than women.

4 In Africa, people speak more than 2,000 languages. In North and South America, people speak almost 1,000 languages. People in Africa speak **more** / **less** languages than people in North and South America.

5 In Mexico, the dog is a **more** / **less** popular pet than a parakeet. People like parakeets more than dogs.

6 In India, 946 films are made per year. In the U.S.A., 611 films are made per year. The U.S.A. makes **more** / **fewer** films per year than India.

10 **Answer the questions. Write complete sentences.**

1 Do you watch more or fewer hours of TV a week than people in the U.S.A.?

_____

2 In your country, is a rabbit a more popular pet than a cat?

_____

3 Do you think your country makes fewer or more films a year than the U.S.A.?

_____

4 Do you think your country has more or less people than the U.S.A.?

_____

5 In your class, are there more girls or boys?

_____

How did I do? ☆☆☆☆☆

The Amazon rain forest has **the most** species of plants and animals on Earth.
Germany and Switzerland have **the fewest** pet dogs per capita.
Which country has **the least** amount of air pollution?

11 **Draw lines to connect the sentence parts.**

1 A tree in Nevada, in the
U.S.A., is 4,800 years old.
It is

the least

tourists of
any city in Mexico.

2 Mexico City has more
than 20 million tourists
each year. It has

the longest

mammal in the world.

3 The kakapo parrot
weighs 3.5 kilograms.
It is

the oldest

amount of rain a year of
all deserts.

4 It rarely rains in the
Atacama Desert in Chile.
It has

the lightest

parrot in the world.

5 Siberia has a very long
railway. It has

the heaviest

railway in the world.

6 The bumblebee bat only
weighs two grams. It is

the most

tree alive.

12 **Read the answers and write the questions.**

1 Which species is one of the most endangered species in the Americas?

The armadillo is one of the most endangered species in the Americas.

2 _____

The piranha has the sharpest teeth of all fish.

3 _____

The white millipede has the most legs of any animal. It has a total of 750 wiggling legs!

4 _____

The land mammal with the fewest teeth is the narwhal. It has only two, large teeth.

How did I do? ☆☆☆☆☆

13 **Read and complete. Then listen and check.**

| water | pitcher plant | nectar | nutrients | absorbs | slippery | insects |

How to Take Care of a Pitcher Plant

Do you want to have a pet, but your parents won't let you? If your parents won't allow pets in your home, you could try growing a ¹_____. It could be your perfect "pet plant!" You can take care of it and feed it just like a pet. But be careful. At mealtimes, these plants get very hungry!

Pitcher plants need lots of ²_____ and protein. To be a good pitcher plant owner, you'll have to make sure that your plant gets lots of sunlight and ³_____. These are important to keep your little carnivore happy and healthy. Water's especially important. It makes the top of the plant ⁴_____ so that insects can slip into the nectar. The plant is shaped like a cup, so insects are easily trapped in it. The sweet-smelling, sticky ⁵_____ helps the plant digest the food. The plant then uses chemicals to break down the proteins and nutrients in the food, and ⁶_____ them.

Check your plant to make sure it's catching enough ⁷_____. Some days you'll have to feed it an extra insect or two if it looks hungry. Your pitcher plant will have the healthiest and happiest pet plant life of all if you love it and take good care of it.

14 **Read 13 again and answer the questions.**

1 Why is the pitcher plant like a pet?

_____

2 How can you keep a pitcher plant healthy?

_____

3 What does a pitcher plant need to catch its food?

_____

4 What does a pitcher plant eat?

_____

How did I do? ☆☆☆☆☆

15 **Listen and read. Which ancient civilization should you thank for things you have today? Write The Aztecs, The Incas, or The Greeks.**

WHICH CIVILIZATION?

1 _____

This ancient civilization has had a very important influence on the modern world. For example, your favorite athletes can compete to be the best in the world at the Olympic Games, thanks to this ancient culture. When you get bored, you can read incredible stories about heroes, gods, and goddesses, too, as this culture has left us with an amazing legacy of literature.

2 _____

This ancient civilization gave us a type of farming that is still practiced today in many countries around the world. For example, the people in Thailand and Vietnam grow rice and other crops on hills using terraced farming. When you get ill, your mom or the doctor might give you herbal remedies to make you feel better. Many of these herbal remedies were also discovered by this ancient civilization.

3 _____

When you get hungry and want something sweet, you might enjoy eating a chocolate bar. You have this ancient civilization to thank for the cultivation of cacao, which is the main ingredient in chocolate. Mmmm… chocolate!

16 **Look at 15. Circle T for true or F for false.**

1	At the Olympic Games, athletes compete to be the best in the world.	T	F
2	Stories about gods and goddesses come from ancient literature.	T	F
3	The Ancient Greeks influenced modern culture.	T	F
4	Thai and Vietnamese farmers grow their crops on flat land.	T	F
5	People may use herbal remedies when they are ill.	T	F
6	The Incas used a method of farming which isn't used today.	T	F
7	Cacao is not the main ingredient in chocolate.	T	F
8	The Aztecs left us with a legacy of literature.	T	F
9	The Incas developed the chocolate bar.	T	F

How did I do? ☆ ☆ ☆ ☆ ☆

A play tells a story. Both a play and a story have...

• characters

• important events

• an order of events

But a play is a special kind of story. It tells the story through dialogs, and actors speaking those dialogs. The dialogs show what the people want, what they're thinking, and what's happening or has happened. The dialog is the only thing that tells us about the characters and events.

17 **Read the story of Daedalus and Icarus in 5 again. Answer the questions.**

1 How many characters are there in the story?

_____

2 What are the names of the characters?

_____

3 How would you describe each of the characters?

_____

4 There are three events mentioned in the story.

What happened first? _____

What happened second? _____

What happened in the end? _____

5 What do these characters say, think, or wish in the story?

King Minos: _____

Daedalus: _____

Icarus: _____

18 **Choose one of the events in 17. Rewrite the event as a play in your notebook.**

How did I do? ☆ ☆ ☆ ☆ ☆

Review

19 **Read and match. Write the letters.**

____ **1** In English, we have to read

____ **2** For math, he mustn't forget

____ **3** In science class, they have to

____ **4** In history, I must do

a work in groups to do the experiment.

b my own research about ancient Greece.

c to bring his homework.

d a poem by Shakespeare.

20 **Read and complete the sentences.**

1 A spider has eight legs. An ant has six legs.

A spider has _____ than an ant.

2 I have two pets. My friend Alex has three pets.

I have _____ than Alex.

3 London has about eight million people. Birmingham has about one million people.

London has _____ than Birmingham.

4 My pitcher plant eats four insects a day. Your pitcher plant eats six insects a day.

My pitcher plant eats _____ than yours.

21 **Complete the sentences. Use the least, the fewest, or the most and the underlined words.**

1 Children in Finland don't <u>do</u> much <u>homework</u>.

They _____ of any European country.

2 France <u>has</u> a lot of <u>pet owners</u>.

It _____ of any European country.

3 Canada <u>has</u> a small number of <u>mammals</u>.

It _____ of any country in the world.

4 Approximately 32 percent of families in the U.S.A. <u>own dogs</u>. That's more than any other country.

They _____ of any country in the world.

How did I do? ☆☆☆☆☆

 Write about yourself. Look at Units 4, 5, and 6 to help you.

My Dreams for the Future

_____

_____

_____

_____

Super Powers I Want

_____

_____

_____

_____

My School Interests

_____

_____

_____

_____

2 Make a list of your superheroes –
real or imaginary.

3 Look at 2. Choose one superhero and
make some notes about your choice.

His/Her Dreams

_____

_____

_____

His/Her Powers

_____

_____

_____

His/Her Interests

_____

_____

_____

4 Look at 2 and 3. Write a song about your superhero. Use some of these
sentences in your song. Add your own sentences.

I'll save my best numbers for you.

If I could fly like Superman...

Pow! Bam! Slam! Kaboom!

Superhero, here I am.

I'll be living on the moon.

I've got my super power.

I'll be traveling through time soon.

7 Mysteries!

1 Match the pictures with the explanations of these unsolved mysteries. Do you think these explanations are possible? Circle Possible or Not Possible.

1

2

3

4

a Overnight, the wind creates unusual circles in farmer's fields.　　Possible　　Not Possible

b Giant pre-historic ape-like men still live in the Himalayas of Asia.　　Possible　　Not Possible

c Large, heavy rocks weighing up to 300 kilos move from place to place by themselves.　　Possible　　Not Possible

d Aliens from outer space created perfectly round sculptures in Costa Rica.　　Possible　　Not Possible

2 **Complete the dialogs. Then listen and check your answers.**

> explanation   Great Pyramids   Northern Lights
> scientific proof   theories   unsolved

A: Have you ever heard of the ¹_____?

B: Yes, I think so. They're those bright, colorful lights in the night sky. They're caused by light reflecting off the ice caps in the Arctic.

A: No, that was just a theory. Now there's ²_____. Gases in the air cause these nighttime fireworks.

A: The ³_____ in Egypt are incredible, aren't they?

B: They certainly are. Does anyone have an ⁴_____ of how they were built?

A: Well, some scientists have ⁵_____ about it, but the mystery is still ⁶_____.

3 **Read the sentences about the places in 2. Circle T for true or F for false. Correct the false sentences.**

1 The Great Pyramids are an unsolved mystery, but scientists have some theories about them.   T   F

_____

2 There is scientific proof about how the Great Pyramids were built.   T   F

_____

3 The Northern Lights appear in the night sky over Egypt.   T   F

_____

THINK BIG

Do you think that most mysteries can be explained by science? Why/Why not?

_____

4 **Listen and read. Then answer the questions.**

The Voynich Manuscript

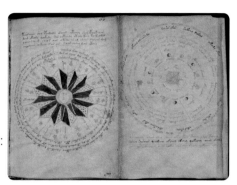

The Voynich Manuscript, written in the 15th century in Western Europe, is beautiful to look at. The pages of this "book" are full of colorful, lovely drawings of plants and astronomical objects, like suns and moons. The handwriting that surrounds the drawings appears to describe herbal remedies from plants. You can imagine that the author was a doctor or a scientist. But if you look more closely, you'll notice two very strange things: the words aren't in any known language and the plants don't exist. That's incredible, isn't it?

Scientists have studied the Voynich Manuscript for years and have tried to understand the meaning of the words and the strange drawings. The words do follow some "rules" of a language, or even two languages, but scientists still cannot work out what the language is. And they don't know where the author learned about the strange plants. An early theory was that the writer used an artificial language. Another theory was that the whole thing was a hoax. But why would someone spend so much time on a manuscript and work so hard if it was just a prank?

Today, a group of scientists from around the world are working together to create a machine that will help them finally crack the code. What do you think? Will a computer be able to help them understand the information that the 15th-century writer so beautifully and carefully put into this manuscript?

COMMENTS (2)

Savvy Sam

This is fascinating! What theories do scientists have about the plants? Could the plants be extinct species? They're amazing!

Georgina

I agree with Savvy Sam. The plants are amazing. I wonder if the plants look different because they're ancient? Plants could change over time, couldn't they? I hope scientists crack the code soon. Maybe the manuscript contains the cure for today's diseases. You never know!

1 How old is the Voynich Manuscript?

_____

2 What's strange about the Voynich Manuscript?

_____

How did I do? ☆ ☆ ☆ ☆ ☆

Language in Action

103

5 Listen and read. Then circle T for true or F for false.

Tony: I got you <u>hooked on</u> *Kryptos*, didn't I?

Gerald: You really did! I found lots of <u>cool stuff</u> about *Kryptos* online. Did you know that the creator of the codes has given more clues recently?

Tony: Seriously? What are the new clues?

Gerald: He gave six letters out of the 97 in the last phrase.

Tony: I bet the decoders got excited, didn't they?

Gerald: <u>Absolutely</u>. On the sculpture, the letters are *NYPVTT*. When decoded, the letters read *BERLIN*.

Tony: I can't imagine being a code breaker, can you? I wouldn't be able to sleep because I'd be thinking about it all the time.

Gerald: That's exactly what's happening. Lots of people are obsessed with cracking the code, and that's all they can think about every day.

Tony: <u>That's ridiculous!</u>

1 Gerald is really interested in *Kryptos*.   T   F

2 Gerald found out about *Kryptos* before Tony.   T   F

3 Tony knew about the new clues that the creator gave out.   T   F

6 Look at **5**. Read the underlined expressions. Match the expressions with their meanings. Write the letters.

___ **1** Hooked on...

___ **2** Cool stuff.

___ **3** Absolutely.

___ **4** That's ridiculous!

a I agree with you completely.

b That's crazy! It's unreasonable.

c Obesessed with something.

d Interesting things.

104

7 Complete with the expressions in **6**. Then listen and check.

1 **A:** Jennifer's always reading.

   B: I know. She's _____ historical mysteries. She reads all day, every day!

   A: Really? _____!

2 **A:** There's a craft fair on Saturday. Let's go. They always have such _____, don't they?

   B: _____. I could buy everything. Great idea!

How did I do? ☆☆☆☆☆

Grammar

AFFIRMATIVE STATEMENTS	NEGATIVE TAGS	NEGATIVE STATEMENTS	POSITIVE TAGS
The geoglyphs **are** in Peru,	**aren't** they?	Atlantis **isn't** real,	**is** it?
Experts **can** explain them,	**can't** they?	Scientists **can't** find it,	**can** they?
We **love** mysteries,	**don't** we?	It **doesn't** make sense,	**does** it?

8 Complete the sentences with question tags.

1 The Voynich Manuscript is a mystery, _____?

2 The plants in the manuscript aren't real species, _____?

3 Scientists can't figure out the language in the manuscript, _____?

4 The pictures of the plants are beautiful, _____?

5 The manuscript isn't a hoax, _____?

6 People can find a lot of information about the Voynich Manuscript online, _____?

9 Complete the sentences with question tags.

1 Scientists can't explain the crop circles in England, _____?

2 The crop circles are perfect geometric patterns, _____?

3 The crop circle appears in fields overnight, _____?

4 There isn't any proof that aliens created crop circles, _____?

How did I do? ☆ ☆ ☆ ☆ ☆

10 **Unscramble the sentences with question tags.**

1 don't / some people / in the Bermuda Triangle / do / believe / they

   Some people don't believe in the Bermuda Triangle, do they?

2 don't / a mysterious / people / phenomenon / love / they

   _____

3 didn't / the Nazca Lines / learned / we / a lot about / my classmates and I

   _____

4 didn't / a theory for the Sailing Stones / did / scientists / have / for a long time / they

   _____

5 seem / the city of Atlantis / does / doesn't / real / it

   _____

11 **Zack is writing a play about Atlantis. Complete the dialog with the question tags in the box.**

| didn't they?   don't we?   do they?   isn't it?   wasn't he?   were they? |

Tabitha: Well, here we are in the city of Atlantis! Wow! It's so cool, ¹_____

Bryan: Yeah. Look at that huge water fountain! It's beautiful!

Tabitha: We look a little funny wearing jeans and a T-shirt, ²_____

Bryan: I told you that we would look strange. Look at that wall. It's covered in gold and silver!

Tabitha: All the walls are covered in metals. Scientists don't really know why this place disappeared, ³_____

Bryan: No, but Plato seemed to know. He said that the gods destroyed Atlantis.

Tabitha: Right. The people weren't good, ⁴_____ So, the gods destroyed the city with an earthquake and giant waves, ⁵_____

Bryan: That's right. Hey, look at that hill. Why is there a hill in the middle of the city?

Tabitha: Look at the top.

Bryan: Oh, that's right. That's the temple of Poseidon. He was a very scary god, ⁶_____

Tabitha: Totally. It sure is fun to travel back in time.

How did I do? ☆☆☆☆☆

106

12 **Read and complete the text with the words in the box. Then listen and check.**

| solar wind | phenomenon | swirling | oxygen | nitrogen |

What Causes the Aurora Borealis?

The Aurora Borealis or "Northern Lights", whose colors light up the night sky, is one of the most beautiful phenomena on Earth. It is also one of the most mystifying since the display of shimmering colors, lines, and shapes is different every time it appears. In the past, there were various theories explaining the appearance of this beautiful **1**_____ display. For example, long ago in Finland, people thought the lights came from a mystical fox flashing its tail in the sky. Over the years, different myths have been told to explain this extraordinary **2**_____ that may be best seen during the winter months in the Arctic. The Aurora Borealis continues to inspire writers, artists, and musicians today.

However, in 2008, scientists developed a theory that everyone could agree on. The spectacular lights were caused by the **3**_____ blowing around ions, atoms, gases, and other things in the atmosphere and making them collide. When they collide, they produce the colorful displays of light. So, how does it actually happen?

The hot solar winds from the sun are blowing oxygen and nitrogen atoms around. There are two kinds of nitrogen atoms – the neutral and the ionic. The atoms are full of energy. When they collide, they give off colors. **4**_____ produces a yellow-green to brownish red color. The neutral nitrogen atoms produce purple and red colors. The ionic **5**_____ atoms produce blue colors.

13 **Read 12 again and choose the correct answers.**

1 Each time the Aurora Borealis appears, it looks _____.

 a different   **b** the same

2 In the past, people in Finland thought the Aurora Borealis was a mystical _____ in the sky.

 a fire   **b** fox

3 Scientists discovered that the Northern Lights were caused by _____ blowing around gases in the atmosphere.

 a strong winds   **b** solar winds

4 When neutral nitrogen atoms collide, they produce _____.

 a red and purple colors   **b** blue colors

How did I do? ☆☆☆☆☆

Read and circle the correct answers.

1 an occasion when someone sees something rare or unusual

   a region   **b** sighting

2 things that show something is real or true

   a proof   **b** samples

3 something someone does to trick or deceive people

   a hoax   **b** myth

4 an object from the past

   a artifact   **b** evidence

108
15 **Listen and read. Then circle T for true or F for false.**

Huge, Hairy Ape-like Creatures: Real or Hoax?

All around the world, there are stories of strange sightings, amazing phenomena, and incredible artifacts. There are myths and legends to explain them, and some have inspired writers, poets, and artists. Researchers have tried to find scientific evidence to explain these mysteries in an attempt to discover whether they are real or just a hoax. The yeti (also known as the abominable snowman, Bigfoot, or Sasquatch) is one such example.

Huge, hairy, ape-like creatures have been the "stars" of at least ten films in Hollywood over the years. In some films, the creature is friendly and huggable like a teddy bear. In other films, it's a terrifying beast that wants to destroy everyone and everything. In real life, this creature has several names, depending on the region of the world in which it's seen. In the United States and Canada, the creature is called Bigfoot or Sasquatch. In the Himalayan regions of Asia, it's called the yeti or the abominable snowman. The color of the fur may be different (the yeti usually has white fur and Bigfoot has dark brown or black), but they both appear to be up to 2.7 meters tall and weigh from 300 to 400 kilos. Their feet can be as large as 43 centimeters long. But are these creatures real?

For years, scientists have thought that these creatures were a hoax, but to this day people continue to claim they've seen them. In 2012, there were many sightings in the United States. One person posted his video on YouTube and the video was seen more than 2 million times.

1 The abominable snowman has never been in a movie.   T   F

2 In Canada the creature is called Sasquatch.   T   F

3 Yetis have white fur.   T   F

4 People don't believe in Bigfoot anymore.   T   F

How did I do?

One purpose for writing is to explain something. When you write a cause-and-effect paragraph, you explain why something happens.

• Why something happens is called a cause.

• The thing that happens is called an effect.

For example, the Aurora Borealis is a beautiful display of lights. The beautiful lights are an effect. Why do the lights happen? That's the cause.

16 Read the paragraph. <u>Underline</u> the causes. (Circle) the effects.

> The Aurora Borealis is a brilliant light show. Colored bands of light paint the night sky in certain parts of the world. What makes this happen? Solar winds interact with the upper part of the atmosphere, causing atoms of oxygen and nitrogen to become changed. As the atoms return to their normal state, they give off colors.

17 Write a cause-and-effect paragraph about something that's happened to you or something you've read about in your science lessons. Use the chart below to organize your ideas.

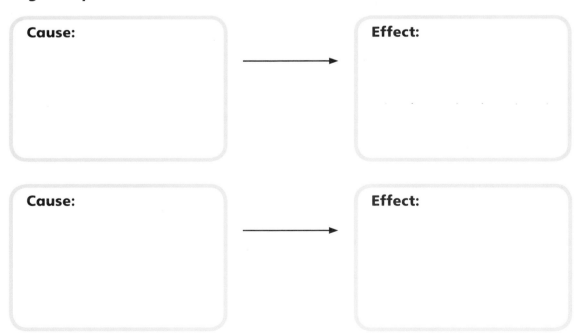

Cause:

Effect:

Cause:

Effect:

How did I do? ☆ ☆ ☆ ☆ ☆

Review

18 **Read and choose the correct answers.**

1 There is no ___ for planes and boats disappearing in the Bermuda Triangle.

    a explanation   **b** phenomenon

2 Scientists know how the Sailing Stones move. That mystery is ___.

    a solved   **b** unsolved

3 Scientists think that crop circles are a hoax. This is a ___.

    a proof   **b** theory

4 Code breakers won't stop trying to crack the code until they have ___ proof that the Voynich Manuscript really is a hoax.

    a solved   **b** scientific

19 **Correct the question tags.**

1 The Aurora Borealis is a phenomenon in the northern hemisphere, is it?

_____

2 The yeti lives in the Himalayas in Asia, isn't it?

_____

3 There isn't proof that the Sailing Stones are real, aren't there?

_____

4 Anyone can read the *Kryptos* codes, didn't they?

_____

20 **Complete the dialogs. Use question tags. Use the information you have learned about mysteries.**

1 **A:** _____?

    B: I don't know. But I would love to know more about this mystery!

2 **A:** _____?

    B: Yes. It's an interesting phenomenon, isn't it?

How did I do? ☆☆☆☆☆

8 Why Is It Famous?

Language in Context

1 **Match the pictures of famous places with the sentences. Why do you think these places are famous? Circle A for architecture, B for natural beauty, or C for mystery. You can circle more than one.**

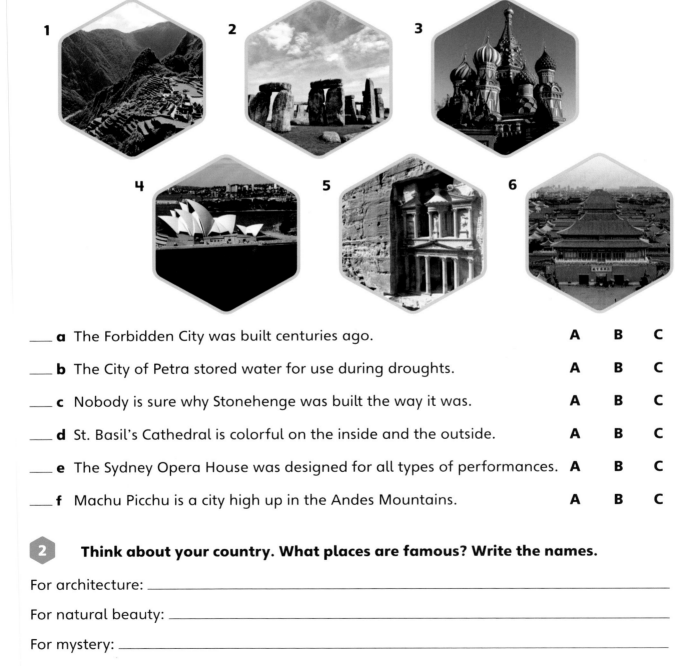

___ **a** The Forbidden City was built centuries ago.   **A**   **B**   **C**

___ **b** The City of Petra stored water for use during droughts.   **A**   **B**   **C**

___ **c** Nobody is sure why Stonehenge was built the way it was.   **A**   **B**   **C**

___ **d** St. Basil's Cathedral is colorful on the inside and the outside.   **A**   **B**   **C**

___ **e** The Sydney Opera House was designed for all types of performances.   **A**   **B**   **C**

___ **f** Machu Picchu is a city high up in the Andes Mountains.   **A**   **B**   **C**

2 **Think about your country. What places are famous? Write the names.**

For architecture: _____

For natural beauty: _____

For mystery: _____

3 Listen and label the pictures with the words in the box.

mausoleum	monument	pyramid	statue	temple	tower

1 _____

2 _____

3 _____

4 _____

5 _____

6 _____

4 Look at 3 and answer the questions.

1 If your class could travel to one of the places or structures, which one would you like to see?

_____

2 Have you ever visited a historic place like those in the pictures? What do you remember most about that place?

_____

_____

Does a landmark have to be old to be famous? Why/Why not?

_____

_____

How did I do? ☆☆☆☆☆

5 **Listen and read. Then answer the questions.**

The Forbidden City

In the middle of Beijing, China, is the magnificent Forbidden City. Although now a museum and officially renamed the Palace Museum, or "Gugong" in Chinese, the Forbidden City was built in the early 1400s by Emperor Yongle as his imperial home. With 90 palaces and over 900 buildings, the Forbidden City was home to 24 Chinese emperors of the Ming and Qing dynasty for almost 500 years.

The Forbidden City is protected by a moat and a wall that is almost eight meters high. There is an inner court with buildings and rooms for the emperor and his family and an outer court with halls and gardens where the emperor did his work and entertained guests. Only people invited by the emperor were allowed into the palace. All others were forbidden to enter.

In front of the main gate, there is a pair of bronze lions. The male lion is holding a globe, symbolizing the power of the emperor. The female lion has a cub. She symbolizes the health and happiness of the emperor's family.

The colors yellow and red appear everywhere. Roofs of the buildings and bricks of the floor are yellow. Yellow symbolized the royal family and its supreme importance to the world. Doors, windows, pillars, and walls were often red. Red symbolized happiness and celebration.

Today, people come from all over the world to see the thousands of items in the Palace Museum; paintings, ceramics, jade pieces, clocks, jewelry, and sculptures all give us a glimpse of history. In 1987, the United Nations Educational, Scientific, and Cultural Organization (UNESCO) included the Forbidden City on its World Heritage List for its incredible architectural beauty and wealth of cultural artifacts.

1 When was the Forbidden City built? Why was it built?

_____

2 Why do you think the emperor's palace was called the Forbidden City?

_____

3 There are statues of lions in front of the main gate. If you lived in a place like the Forbidden City, what animal statues would you have in front of your main gate? Why?

_____

4 The colors red and yellow appear everywhere in the Forbidden City. If you lived in a place like the Forbidden City, what two colors would you use? What would they symbolize?

_____

How did I do? ☆☆☆☆☆

Language in Action

6 Listen and read. Then answer the question.

Tania: Hi, Eric! You're from Australia, aren't you?

Eric: Yes, I was born in Sydney. Why?

Tania: Well, I have to give a presentation in my art class. What do you know about the Sydney Opera House?

Eric: Quite a lot, actually. Did you know that the Opera House <u>is known for</u> its design?

Tania: Hmm. <u>That makes sense.</u> I've seen pictures and it's amazing, isn't it?

Eric: Yeah, it's <u>a work of art</u>! I don't know who designed it, but I do know where the person was from. A design contest <u>was held</u> sometime in the 1950s and the person who won was from Denmark.

Tania: Really? You know, it looks like a big boat, doesn't it?

Eric: Yeah, I've heard other people say the same thing. It's amazing!

Tania: Thanks, Eric. You've given me a good start.

Do Tania and Eric like the design of the Opera House? How do you know?

_____

7 Look at 6. Read the underlined expressions. Match the expressions with their meanings. Write the letters.

___ **1** known for

___ **2** That makes sense.

___ **3** work of art

___ **4** was held

a happened or took place

b painting, sculpture, or object that is skillfully made

c famous for

d That's logical. It's easy to understand.

8 Complete with three of the expressions in 7. Then listen and check. 121

1 A: My family is going to the city of Cambridge this weekend.

B: Really? I've heard of it, but I don't know much about it.

A: It's _____ its architecture and its university, of course. You should go!

2 A: How was your holiday in Paris?

B: Great! We saw the Eiffel Tower. It's a phenomenal _____!

3 A: I'm doing research on Machu Picchu since we're going there on our next vacation.

B: _____.

How did I do? ☆☆☆☆☆

Grammar

Active	Passive
Archeologists discovered Machu Picchu in 1911.	Machu Picchu **was discovered** in 1911 (by archeologists).

9 **Complete the sentences. Use is or are and the correct form of the verb in parentheses.**

1 The Galapagos Islands _____are known_____ (know) for their unique variety of animal and plant species.

2 The Forbidden City _____ (fill) with beautiful paintings and artifacts.

3 The Taj Mahal _____ (make) of marble.

4 The walls of the Taj Mahal _____ (decorate) with many floral designs.

5 The inside walls of St. Basil's Cathedral _____ (paint) every few years.

6 The Sydney Opera House _____ (locate) in Australia.

10 **Write A for active or P for passive next to each sentence.**

___ 1 Easter Island was discovered by Dutch explorers in 1722.

___ 2 The statues on Easter Island are called moai.

___ 3 The moai statues were moved by the Rapa Nui people.

___ 4 Ivan the Terrible built St. Basil's Cathedral in Moscow in the mid-16th century.

11 **Write sentences with the passive form of the verb.**

1 The pyramid at Kukulcán / call / El Castillo

_____

2 Some of the stones of Stonehenge / rebuild / in the early 20th century

_____

3 The Statue of Liberty / give / to the U.S.A. as a gift

_____

How did I do? ☆ ☆ ☆ ☆ ☆

Leonardo da Vinci is the famous artist and inventor **who painted** the Mona Lisa.
The Eiffel Tower is a landmark **that has become** the symbol of Paris, France.

12 **Complete the sentences with who or that.**

1 The Galapagos Islands are named after the huge tortoises _____ are native to the island.

2 Charles Darwin studied the plants and animals _____ lived on the Galapagos Islands in the early 1800s.

3 It was Charles Darwin _____ made the islands famous.

4 The tortoises and lizards are not afraid of the visitors _____ come to see them.

5 The animal _____ is the best-known of all is the Galapagos Tortoise.

13 **Read and match. Write the letters.**

b 1 Machu Picchu is an ancient city.

2 Many tourists get to Machu Picchu by walking on paths.

3 Scientists don't know much about the Incas.

4 Scientists know about the Spanish conquerors.

a They invaded the city in the 1500s.

b The city was built high in the Andes Mountains.

c The Incas lived in Machu Picchu long ago.

d The paths lead to the ancient city.

14 **Look at 13. Rewrite the matching sentences as one sentence.**

1 Machu Picchu is an ancient city that was built high in the Andes Mountains.

2 _____

3 _____

4 _____

How did I do? ☆☆☆☆☆

15 **Read and circle the correct answers.**

1 Someone who studies the remains left by people living long ago.

a archeologist   **b** scientist

2 A collection of valuable things such as gold, silver, and jewels.

a remains   **b** treasure

3 To make a hole in the ground.

a bury   **b** dig

4 An object from the past, such as a tool or a weapon.

a tomb   **b** artifact

16 **Listen and read. Then circle T for true or F for false.**

ACCIDENTAL DISCOVERIES

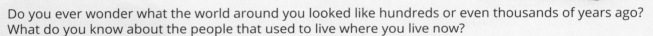

Do you ever wonder what the world around you looked like hundreds or even thousands of years ago? What do you know about the people that used to live where you live now?

There were probably children just like you, who played in the places that you play in today. Below your feet there could be artifacts or even treasures from those times and you could discover them – even by accident. Not all discoveries are made by archeologists, who may spend years researching ancient places. Some discoveries are made accidentally by people just like you.

One important accidental discovery occurred in 1992, in England. A farmer was working in the fields when he lost his hammer. He asked a neighbor to help him find it. His neighbor had a metal detector. The first thing the metal detector found was a silver spoon. Then it found some jewelry and gold coins. The surprised farmers asked for the help of archeologists. When the archeologists excavated, they were shocked to discover a large box with over 14,000 Roman gold and silver coins inside. They believed that the treasure came from the 4th and 5th centuries AD. The archeologists found other artifacts as well, including the farmer's hammer. The artifacts were sold to museums and the farmers received 2.5 million pounds as payment! Now, wasn't this an amazing accidental discovery?

1 The farmer found a tomb.   T   F

2 The first thing found was a silver spoon.   T   F

3 The artifacts were sold to an archeologist.   T   F

4 The farmer was looking for a hammer.   T   F

5 The hammer was never found.   T   F

How did I do? ☆ ☆ ☆ ☆ ☆

125

17 **Read and complete using the words in the box. Then listen and check.**

children	cultures	exist	hope	wonders

The New Seven Wonders of the World

Do you know what the seven wonders of the world are? Over the years, there have been several different lists and many people around the world think they know what the wonders are, but they are not always correct.

A Swiss adventurer, Bernard Weber, decided to create a new list of world
¹_____. He began the New 7 Wonders Foundation. This time, he wanted people from all around the world to choose seven new wonders that ²_____ today. He asked people to send in their votes for the new wonders. People voted by texting, voting online on the website, or calling in their votes. By 2007, more than 100 million people had voted. Who were these voters? Most of the voters were not adults. Bernard Weber is proud of the fact that they were mostly ³_____ and young people.

Weber and a group of people reviewed all the votes. They chose the new seven wonders based on these criteria:

* The places should each have a unique beauty.
* The places should come from all over the world and represent people from all over the world.
* The places should be from different environments, such as deserts and rain forests.
* The places should be important to people from different ⁴_____.
* The places should be located on different continents.

Weber was delighted by the enthusiasm and love that people showed for their cultures and other cultures. This enthusiasm and love, he believes, creates a feeling of ⁵_____ for the future.

18 **Read 17 again and answer the questions.**

1 How many wonders of the world are there?

_____

2 Who began the New 7 Wonders Foundation?

_____

3 Who voted for the new seven wonders?

_____

4 What does Weber say creates a feeling of hope for the future?

_____

How did I do? ☆ ☆ ☆ ☆ ☆

When you do research for a report, use an idea web to organize the information into categories. For example, if you write about a country, make categories for its location, population, and important cities.

When you write, make sure that you write only about one category of information in each paragraph.

19 **Look at the facts. Write the number of each fact in the correct category.**

1 between Pakistan and Burma

2 Kolkata, Chennai, Bangalore, Mumbai

3 southern Asia

4 Hindi

5 English – important language

6 New Delhi – capital city

7 one billion people

8 seventh largest country in the world

The Republic of India

General Facts and Location
_____
_____
_____

Population, People, and Languages
_____
_____
_____

Major Cities
_____
_____
_____

20 **The paragraph below should only include general facts and information about the location of India. Circle the two sentences that do NOT belong in the paragraph.**

The Republic of India is the seventh largest country in the world. It's located in southern Asia. Hindi is its national language. It's situated between Pakistan and Burma. English is an important language, too.

21 **Write a report about India in your notebook. Use the information in 19 and 20.**

How did I do? ☆☆☆☆☆

Review

22   **Circle the correct answers.**

1   A ___ is a place that is built for someone who has died.

    a tower   **b** mausoleum

2   The Great ___ of China was built to keep enemies out.

    a Wall   **b** Statue

3   A ___ is a place for kings or emperors to live.

    a cathedral   **b** palace

4   St. Basil's ___ is in Russia.

    a Tower   **b** Cathedral

23   **Complete the statements with the correct passive form of the verbs in the box.**

> build   discover   locate   make

1   The Temple of Borobudur _____ by thousands of workers between 750 and 850 AD.

2   The Taj Mahal _____ in Agra, India.

3   The Taj Mahal _____ of white marble.

4   Victoria Falls _____ by David Livingstone in 1855.

24   **Combine the sentences. Use that or who and the sentences in the box.**

> They belonged to King Tut.   They lived on Easter Island.

1   The Rapa Nui were Polynesian people.

_____.

2   In the Cairo Museum in Egypt there are artifacts.

_____.

How did I do? ☆ ☆ ☆ ☆ ☆

9 That's Entertainment!

Language in Context

1 **Read the statements and ✔ the ones that describe you.**

1 ☐ Music is very important in my life.
2 ☐ Reading is very important in my life.
3 ☐ Video games are very important in my life.
4 ☐ Movies are very important in my life.
5 ☐ I like to read about singers and actors.
6 ☐ I like animation more than regular movies.
7 ☐ I like movies that scare me.
8 ☐ I like to talk about the concerts I go to.

2 **Read and circle the answers that are true for you.**

	Sometimes	Often	Never
1 I go to the movie theater.	S	O	N
2 I go to concerts.	S	O	N
3 I go to bookstores or the library.	S	O	N
4 I go to festivals to see people perform.	S	O	N
5 I watch movie award shows on TV.	S	O	N
6 I watch music contests on TV.	S	O	N
7 I read when I get bored.	S	O	N
8 I play video games when I get bored.	S	O	N

3 **Complete the sentences with the words in the box.**

> book signing   comic book exhibit   concert
> festival   movie premiere   video game launch

1 People are walking around dressed up as *Star Wars* storm troopers, *Avatar* characters, and Mario. There are cool books, posters, T-shirts, and hats for sale. Going to a _____ is so much fun!

2 People are standing in line waiting until midnight to get into the store. Everybody wants to be the first to own the new game. This _____ is the best!

3 The place is full of people dancing and singing along with the performer on stage. The music is really loud! The tickets were expensive but worth it to see this singer in _____!

4 Photographers are taking pictures of the actors as they walk into the movie theater. People are so excited to see their favorite stars! Being at a _____ is incredible!

5 The author of the latest best-selling book is sitting behind a table. People are standing in line holding the book. A _____ is really fun to go to.

6 Thousands of people have come to see the dancers dressed in stunning traditional costumes dancing to folk music. People are in a wonderful mood for these two days at the _____.

THINK BIG

If you went to a comic book exhibit and you could dress as any character, which character would you be? Why?

_____

_____

132

4 Read and listen. Then circle the correct names.

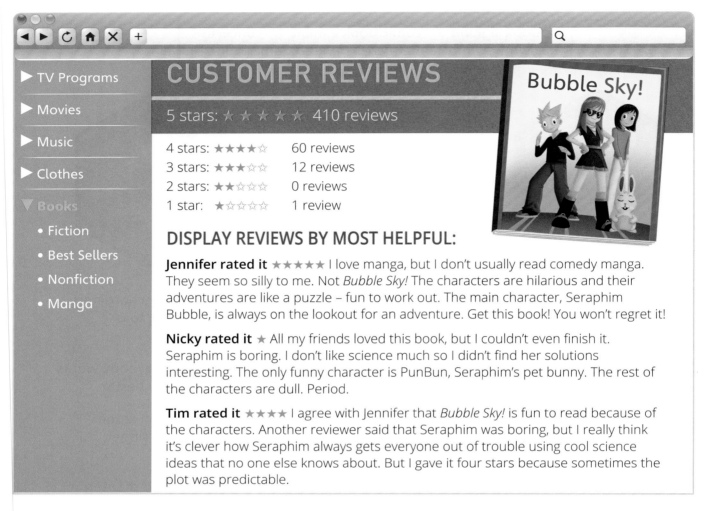

▶ TV Programs
▶ Movies
▶ Music
▶ Clothes
▼ Books
• Fiction
• Best Sellers
• Nonfiction
• Manga

CUSTOMER REVIEWS

Bubble Sky!

5 stars: ★ ★ ★ ★ ★   410 reviews

4 stars: ★★★★☆   60 reviews
3 stars: ★★★☆☆   12 reviews
2 stars: ★★☆☆☆   0 reviews
1 star: ★☆☆☆☆   1 review

DISPLAY REVIEWS BY MOST HELPFUL:

Jennifer rated it ★★★★★ I love manga, but I don't usually read comedy manga. They seem so silly to me. Not *Bubble Sky!* The characters are hilarious and their adventures are like a puzzle – fun to work out. The main character, Seraphim Bubble, is always on the lookout for an adventure. Get this book! You won't regret it!

Nicky rated it ★ All my friends loved this book, but I couldn't even finish it. Seraphim is boring. I don't like science much so I didn't find her solutions interesting. The only funny character is PunBun, Seraphim's pet bunny. The rest of the characters are dull. Period.

Tim rated it ★★★★ I agree with Jennifer that *Bubble Sky!* is fun to read because of the characters. Another reviewer said that Seraphim was boring, but I really think it's clever how Seraphim always gets everyone out of trouble using cool science ideas that no one else knows about. But I gave it four stars because sometimes the plot was predictable.

1   **Jennifer / Nicky / Tim** said that the characters were hilarious.

2   **Jennifer / Nicky / Tim** said that all her friends loved the book.

3   **Jennifer / Nicky / Tim** said that the plot was sometimes predictable.

5 Answer the questions.

1   Why did Jennifer like the adventures?

_____

2   Have you ever read manga? What would a manga book need to include for you to give it five stars?

_____

How did I do? ☆ ☆ ☆ ☆ ☆

Language in Action

6 Listen and read. Then answer the questions.

PREMIERE
SPIDER-MAN

Ann: Mom? Um, could I possibly borrow fifteen dollars?

Mom: What for?

Ann: I want to go and see all the celebrities at the movie premiere of *Spider-Man*. All my friends are going. But I don't have enough money for the train.

Mom: What happened to your allowance?

Ann: I spent it on that concert last week. It was more expensive than I thought.

Mom: Well, I suppose I could give you next week's allowance in advance, but that means you won't get anything next week.

Ann: OK. Deal! Thanks, Mom.

1 What does Ann want from her mom?

_____

2 Ann won't get any allowance money next week. Why?

_____

7 Look at 6. Circle the correct answers.

1 When Ann's mom says "What for?", she means ___.

  a Why do you need it?   **b** What do you mean?

2 "In advance" means ___.

  a an increase   **b** early

3 When Ann says "Deal!", she means ___.

  a I agree.   **b** Let's play cards.

8 Complete with two of the expressions in 6. Then listen and check.

John: Do you want to stop at the shopping mall on the way home?

Jim: [1]_____

John: I need some things for my science project.

Jim: OK. But only if we go to the pizza place in there first. I'm so hungry!

John: OK. [2]_____

How did I do? ☆☆☆☆☆

Grammar

Direct speech	Reported speech
Claire said, "The album **isn't** as good as the last one."	Claire/She said (that) the album **wasn't** as good as the last one.
Josh said, "I**'m going** to the premiere."	Josh/He said (that) he **was going** to the premiere.

9 **Read the dialogs and answer the questions. Use reported speech.**

Katie: Hey, Joe! What are you doing tonight?

Joe: I'm going to a live show at Dragon's Den to see Ed Sheeran. What about you?

Katie: I'm not doing anything.

1 What is Joe doing tonight?

He said he was going to a live show at Dragon's Den to see Ed Sheeran.

2 What is Katie doing tonight?

_____

Sam: The new *Play to Win 2* video game is really challenging.

Zena: It's much better than *Play to Win 1*.

3 What did Sam say about *Play to Win 2*?

_____

4 What did Zena say about *Play to Win 2*?

_____

Nina: I want to go to the comic book exhibit!

John: Me, too! I'm going to dress up as Mario.

5 Where did Nina want to go?

_____

6 What did John say?

_____

How did I do? ☆☆☆☆☆

10 **Read the dialog and complete the sentences. Use reported speech.**

> I don't want to miss the book signing at the bookstore today. My mom is taking me.

> I'm so excited. I'm going with my friend to a video game launch today!

1 He _____ said _____ he _____ didn't want _____ to miss the book signing.

2 He _____ his mom _____ him.

3 She _____ she _____ so excited.

4 She _____ she _____ to a video game launch.

11 **Read the dialog and answer the questions. Use reported speech.**

Janet: Hi, Chuck. Where are you going?

Chuck: I'm going to the movies with a friend.

Janet: You're lucky. My friend doesn't want to go with me. I don't want to go alone. But I really want to see the new *Bubble Sky* movie.

Chuck: Come with us.

Janet: Seriously? Thanks!

1 What did Chuck say about his plans?

He said he was going to the movies with a friend.

2 What did Janet say about her friend?

_____ with her.

3 What did she say about going to the movies alone?

_____

4 What did she say she wanted to do?

_____

How did I do? ☆☆☆☆☆

12 **Circle the correct answers.**

1 the characters fix their problem

    a climax   **b** story opening

2 a person who makes movies

    a producer   **b** writer

3 what happens in the story

    a plot   **b** structure

4 the words for the movie

    a climax   **b** script

5 a person who writes stories

    a writer   **b** structure

6 the rules for story writing

    a script   **b** formula

138

13 **Read and complete the text with the words in the box. Then listen and check.**

| review   formula   writing   producers   script   movies |

What's your dream job?

My dream job is to be a **1**_____ writer for Hollywood movies.

I love writing and watching movies. I joined the school newspaper last year, I write a movie

2_____ every week. There are so many different movies, I love finding a new movie to share with

my friends. If you want to watch a great movie, you should read my reviews!

This year I want to start writing my own stories so I'm going to join the writing club. We're going to study

books, plays, and **3**_____ to learn about the skills of being a writer. The first book I'm going to

read is *Save the Cat!* By Blake Snyder. He's a famous script writer in Hollywood, so I'm sure the book will give

me lots of great advice about the **4**_____ for writing my own movie script.

In ten years I'll probably be living in America. I might not be a successful script writer in ten years, but I will

definitely be studying and **5**_____ everyday so I can achieve my goal!

I don't want to be famous, but I want to work with famous actors and movie **6**_____ to make

my stories into amazing movies for my friends to watch.

How did I do? ☆☆☆☆☆

14 Read and complete the text with the words in the box. Then listen and check.

| concerts | flutes | plastic | sounds | unusual |

Unique Musical Instruments

Every culture has musical instruments that are unique to it. The instruments are often made from a variety of materials such as wood, steel, animal bones, and ¹_____. Many people are proud of the musical instruments that are associated with their cultures. Often these instruments make distinctive sounds, too – like no other sound that you've heard before. In Vienna, there's an orchestra that's really unique, because it plays instruments from the things your mother tells you to eat every day. The Vienna Vegetable Orchestra plays instruments made out of vegetables! Can you imagine the unique sounds they make?

The eleven musicians in the Vienna Vegetable Orchestra play carrot ²_____, radish horns, pepper rattlers, carrot trumpets, eggplant clappers, pumpkin bongos, and cucumber phones. The orchestra plays contemporary, jazz, and electronic music, among other styles. They play ³_____ around the world. At the end of their concerts, the members of the audience receive a bowl of vegetable soup to enjoy. So, not only do you get to hear ⁴_____ music, but you get to taste something delicious, too! The third album of the Vienna Vegetable Orchestra is called *Onionoise* and includes songs entitled *Nightshades* and *Transplants*. Can you think of any other suitable titles for their compositions?

Why did this group of visual artists, poets, designers, and writers choose vegetables to create music? They were fascinated by the challenge to produce musical ⁵_____ using natural foods. They constantly experiment with vegetables to create new and complex sounds. As part of their work, they give workshops on how to create instruments from vegetables. A morning TV program said it was "…a highly unusual, tasty performance."

You knew vegetables were good for you. Now you know that they sound good, too! What's your favorite vegetable? Can you think of a musical instrument that you could make out of it?

15 Read **14** again and choose the correct answers.

1 Musical instruments are often made of materials like plastic, steel, wood, and ___.

   a animal feathers   **b** animal bones

2 The Vienna Vegetable Orchestra plays electronic, jazz, and ___.

   a contemporary music   **b** classical music

3 At the end of a concert, a bowl of soup is given to the ___.

   a audience   **b** orchestra

4 The orchestra teaches people how to ___.

   a make soup from vegetables   **b** make instruments from vegetables

How did I do? ☆☆☆☆☆

A good movie review briefly describes the important parts of the movie: the story, the hero and characters, and your opinion (what you liked and didn't like).

Before you write, make a chart that includes these topics and add vivid adjectives such as *stunning*, *captivating*, *tense*, *dull*, and *boring*.

When you write, order your ideas. Write about the story first but don't give away the ending! Some people want the ending to be a surprise. Then write about the characters. Describe them and what they do. Finally, describe what you liked and didn't like (for example, the acting or special effects).

16 **Put the paragraphs in order. Write 1, 2, or 3.**

Review of

BUBBLE SKY: THE MOVIE

____ Some of the acting is fabulous! Melinda Mendez is very good as Seraphim Bubble. Brad Davis is hilarious as Tran. The evil Ms. Doze, played by Vivian Bell, is captivating, but Sandy Dennis as the teacher is dull. The special effects are stunning! All in all, this was a very cool film!

____ *Bubble Sky* is a captivating animation adventure. In the story, a young girl discovers that her school is taken over by aliens. She figures out that a particular herb might destroy them. She needs to find the herb and then get the aliens to eat it.

____ Seraphim Bubble is the hero of the story. Her pet rabbit, PunBun, gives good advice. Seraphim's younger brother Tran and her friend Gayle help her fight the aliens.

17 **Look at 16. Complete the chart about *Bubble Sky*.**

The story	The hero and characters	The opinion (what you liked and didn't like)

18 **Write a review of a movie playing near you this weekend. Make a chart to help you.**

How did I do? ☆☆☆☆☆

Review

19 **Circle the correct events.**

1 The author arrived late for the **movie premiere / book signing**. The manager of the bookstore was upset because people were waiting.

2 My brother and I went to the **comic book exhibit / concert**. We dressed up as Mario and Pikachu. There were thousands of people there.

3 My town is having an arts and crafts **concert / festival**. For three days, painters, potters, and jewelry makers will be selling their work.

4 This Friday night, all the stars will be at the **movie premiere / festival** of the new *Superman* movie.

5 The **concert / video game launch** tickets for *The Eyes* go on sale next Tuesday. They'll sell out fast!

20 **Change the direct speech to reported speech.**

1 Carol said, "I'm tired."

_____

2 Jason said, "I'm going to be at the movie premiere."

_____

3 Diana said, "I want to meet the author of the book."

_____

4 Will said, "I don't really like sci-fi movies."

_____

21 **Change the reported speech to direct speech.**

1 Paolo said he didn't want to go to the festival.
Paolo said, "_____."

2 Lara said she was a pretty good singer.
Lara said, "_____."

3 Harry said he was excited about the comic book exhibit.
Harry said, "_____."

How did I do? ☆☆☆☆☆

Checkpoint | Units 6–9

1 Look at the pictures. Complete the items. Add your own items on the extra lines.

Mysterious Events

1 Northern _____

2 _____ circles

3 Bermuda _____

4 _____

Famous Places

1 _____ of Borobudur

2 _____ of Liberty

3 _____ of Kukulcán

4 _____

Special Events

1 _____ signing

2 rock _____

3 movie _____

4 _____

2 **Find a famous place or event that interests you. Complete the chart.**

Name of the place or event	_____
When was it built, discovered, or found? When did it take place? Where is it located?	_____ _____
Is this a place or event that was mentioned in a song? What's the name of the song? Who's the singer? What are the words (the lyrics) that mention the place?	_____ _____ _____ _____
This place or event was described in a book, online, or in a magazine, wasn't it? What was the title of the book or article? What did the writer say about it?	_____ _____ _____

3 **Do research. Find more information about the place or event in 2. Write a report about it.**

_____

_____

_____

_____

_____

_____

_____

_____

_____

Extra Grammar Practice

1 **Read Julia's plan for her science report. Write questions and answers. Use** yet **and** already**.**

The Importance of the Monarch Butterfly
by Julia Black

Monday	Tuesday	Wednesday	Thursday	Friday
Morning: go to Museum of Natural History, draw Monarch Butterflies Afternoon: write questions about the butterflies	Morning: do research on Monarch Butterflies and answer my questions	Morning: write my report on Monarch Butterflies	Morning: create my presentation	Morning: hand in my report and give presentation

1 It's Monday afternoon.

Q: (Julia / go to the museum) _____

A: _____

2 It's Tuesday.

Q: (she / write her report) _____

A: _____

3 It's Tuesday afternoon.

Q: (she / do her research) _____

A: _____

4 It's Thursday afternoon.

Q: (she / create her presentation) _____

A: _____

5 It's Thursday afternoon.

Q: (she / give her presentation) _____

A: _____

How did I do? ☆ ☆ ☆ ☆ ☆

Extra Grammar Practice

1 **Complete the sentences with the present perfect progressive form of the verbs in parentheses and** for **or** since**.**

1 Jimmy Woodard _____ (take) computers apart _____ he was five years old.

2 Caitlyn _____ (play) chess _____ she was very young.

3 I _____ (collect) stamps _____ two years.

4 Serena _____ (study) martial arts _____ five years.

2 **Ask and answer questions about the chart. Use the present perfect and** for **or** since**.**

Mr. Freedman's Class – Hobbies		
Student	Hobby	How Long?
Rob	collects coins	four years
Cynthia	makes jewelry	she was nine
David	draws cartoon characters	three years
Iris	has dance lessons	six months

1 **Q :** How long _____

A : _____

2 **Q :** How long _____

A : _____

3 **Q** _____

A : _____

4 **Q :** _____

A : _____

How did I do? ☆☆☆☆☆

Extra Grammar Practice

1   **Complete the sentences with the correct form of the verbs in parentheses.**

How will you help your family and friends?

1   If I _____ (finish) my homework early, I'll help with the chores.

2   If my sister doesn't understand her homework, I _____ (help) her.

3   I _____ (call) my friend if he's sick.

4   If my dad _____ (ask) me to walk the dog, I _____ (do) it.

2   **Complete the sentences so they are true for you.**

1   If someone gives me a present, _____.

2   If someone in my family is sick, _____.

3   If my friend gets upset with me, _____.

3   **Read and match. Write the letters.**

Advice to a New Exchange Student at School

___ **1** You're new.

___ **2** Some people are mean to you.

___ **3** You don't speak the language well.

a   Don't worry about your mistakes. Speak anyway.

b   Join clubs so that you meet people.

c   Stay away from those people.

4   **Write the sentences in 3 with should or shouldn't.**

1 _____

2 _____

3 _____

5   **Complete the sentences with your own ideas.**

1 _____, you should ask them to stop.

2 _____, you should apologize.

3 _____, you should get help.

How did I do? ☆☆☆☆☆

Extra Grammar Practice

1 **Look at the chart and circle the correct answers.**

	I like	I don't like
Emily	languages writing and blogging big families living close to family	sports
Al	making money all sports studying hard living in other countries	languages

1 In 10 years, **Emily** / **Al** will definitely be studying languages at college.

2 In 10 years, **Emily** / **Al** probably will be running and hiking at the weekends.

3 In 10 years, **Emily** / **Al** probably won't be living in the same city.

4 In 20 years, **Emily** / **Al** will definitely be earning a good salary.

2 **Write sentences. Use the future progressive and the words in parentheses.**

What will you be doing in 20 years?

1 Celia: I love animals. I don't like living in the city. I like traveling.

    a _____ (I / work as a vet)

    b _____ (I / live in the country)

2 Jeff: I love biology and helping people. I don't like cooking. I like boats.

    a _____ (I / finish medical school)

    b _____ (I / work as a chef)

3 **Answer the questions about yourself. Use No, definitely not, Yes, definitely, Probably not, or Yes, probably.**

1 In seven years will you be at college? _____

2 In two years will you be blogging? _____

How did I do? ☆☆☆☆☆

Extra Grammar Practice

1 **Complete the dialogs with the phrases in the box.**

> join some clubs   start a blog
> start reading fun things like manga comics   have lots of singing lessons

1 Rita: I want to be a singer when I grow up.

  Eddie: If I were you, _____.

2 John: I don't enjoy reading.

  Nancy: If I were you, _____.

3 Tom: I'm bored all the time.

  Kristy: If I were you, _____.

4 Grace: I like writing a lot.

  Sam: If I were you, _____.

2 **Circle the correct verbs.**

1 If you **will get** / **got** up earlier, you **wouldn't be** / **won't be** late for school all the time.

2 If the world **could have** / **can have** superheroes, it **would be** / **was** a safer place to live.

3 If he **practiced** / **will practice** the guitar more, he **will play** / **would play** better.

4 If our chess team **will win** / **won** more matches, we **will compete** / **would compete** in the national championships.

3 **Complete the questions using the words in parentheses. Then answer the questions.**

1 (live / could / you / if / anywhere) _____

_____, where would you live?

I _____.

2 If you could choose your own super powers, (you / choose / which / would)

_____?

I _____.

How did I do? ☆☆☆☆☆

Extra Grammar Practice

1   **Circle the correct words.**

1   Pandas only live in China. Brown bears live in many countries. Pandas live in **more** / **fewer** places than brown bears.

2   Brown bears spend **less** / **more** time eating than pandas. Pandas need to eat lots of bamboo every day to get enough nutrients.

3   Parakeets have **fewer** / **more** legs than dogs.

4   Parakeets eat **more** / **less** food than dogs.

2   **Read the facts. Then complete the sentences using most, least, or fewest and the words in parentheses.**

> **Facts**
> Monserrat has <u>less</u> crime than other countries.
> Greater London has <u>more</u> people than other counties in England.
> Canada has very <u>few</u> species of mammals. It has fewer than any other country.
> People in Papua, New Guinea, speak <u>more</u> languages than people in other countries.
> Taki Taki, the language of Suriname, has <u>few</u> words.

1   Greater London has the _____ (people) of any other county in England.

2   People in Papua, New Guinea, speak the _____ (languages) of any country.

3   Canada has the _____ (species of mammals) of any country.

4   The language of Taki Taki has the _____ (words) of all languages.

5   The country of Monserrat has the _____ (crime) of all countries.

3   **Complete the sentences with the words in the box. Use superlatives.**

1   The sun bear lives in Southeast Asia. It is only 1.2 meters tall. It is _____ in the world.

2   No bird is taller than the ostrich. The ostrich is _____ in the world.

> large / creature
> small / bear
> tall / bird

3   No animal on land is larger than the elephant. The elephant is _____ on land.

How did I do? ☆ ☆ ☆ ☆ ☆

Extra Grammar Practice

1 **Choose the correct words and complete the sentences.**

1 *Kryptos* is a sculpture in the United States, _____ it?

    a is   **b** isn't

2 The fourth section of *Kryptos* isn't solved, _____ it?

    a is   **b** isn't

3 There are many people trying to solve it, _____ there?

    a are   **b** aren't

4 Code breakers can't solve it, _____ they?

    a can   **b** can't

2 **Write question tags to complete the questions.**

1 The Great Pyramids of Egypt are beautiful, _____?

2 The Sailing Stones aren't a mystery any more, _____?

3 The Bermuda Triangle is mysterious, _____?

4 You can climb the pyramids in Mexico, _____?

3 **Unscramble the sentences and add question tags.**

1 found out / scientists / in the early 20th century / about the Nazca Lines

_____

2 the Nazcans created / the lines / don't / scientists / know why

_____

3 drew / the Nazcans / animal and plant figures

_____

4 the lines / need to see / you / from a plane

_____

5 didn't know / you / about the Nazca Lines

_____

How did I do? ☆ ☆ ☆ ☆ ☆

Extra Grammar Practice

1　**Circle the correct verbs.**

1　The *Mona Lisa* **paints** / **was painted** by Leonardo da Vinci.

2　The Taj Mahal **was built** / **built** by the emperor of India.

3　The Statue of Liberty and the Eiffel Tower **were designed** / **designed** by the same French designer.

2　**Write the sentences in the passive.**

1　The people of Egypt built the Great Pyramids of Egypt.

_____

2　Someone moved the Moai statues of Easter Island.

_____

3　**Write sentences in the passive. Use the verbs in the box.**

destroy　　name　　trade

1　The city of Petra, Jordan / one of the seven wonders of the world in 2007

_____

2　Spices, perfumes, and other things / in Petra

_____

3　The city of Petra / by an earthquake in 363 AD

_____

4　**Complete the sentences with the names of places in your country.**

1　_____ is visited every year by thousands of tourists.

2　_____ is known as one of the most beautiful places in my country.

3　_____ is said to be one of the most mysterious places in my country.

How did I do? ☆☆☆☆☆

Extra Grammar Practice

1 **What did the people say about the movie? Rewrite the sentences in reported speech.**

Claire: The acting is incredible.
Jeff: The music is really cool.
Mira: It isn't the director's best movie.
Nancy: It's definitely going to win an Oscar.
Tom: It's not that entertaining.
Ben: The plot is too predictable.

1 Claire _____.

2 Jeff _____.

3 Mira _____.

4 Nancy _____.

5 Tom _____.

6 Ben _____.

2 **Rewrite the sentences in reported speech.**

Tina: I'm going to a Justin Bieber concert for my birthday.
Paul: I'm going to a movie premiere to see Jennifer Lawrence.

1 Tina _____.

2 Paul _____.

Mike: I want to buy the new *Cats* video game.
Sheila: I don't like playing video games.

3 Mike _____.

4 Sheila _____.

Tonya: I'm not going to the book signing.
Freddie: I always go to book signings.

5 She _____.

6 He _____.

How did I do? ☆ ☆ ☆ ☆ ☆

Pearson Education Limited
KAO Two
KAO Park
Harlow
Essex
CMI7 9NA
England
and Associated Companies throughout the world.

www.pearsonelt.com/bigenglish2

First published 2017
Tenth impression 2024

ISBN: 978-1-2922-3337-6

Set in Heinemann Roman
Printed in Slovakia by Neografia

Acknowledgements
The publisher would like to thank the following for their kind permission to reproduce their photographs:

(Key: b-bottom; c-centre; l-left; r-right; t-top)

123RF.com: 7, Andrey Kiselev 64c, ktsdesign 40b, Dmitriy Shironosov 43, Cathy Yeulet 22/2, 31; **Alamy Stock Photo:** Akademie 55b, 63, Art Collection 2 68tr, Sabena Jane Blackbird 66/1, Blend Images 8tr, 34c/5, 54/2, blickwinkel 34cl/5, 66/3, 101b, Michel Platini Fernandes Borges 11, Design Pics Inc 2/3, 4b, dieKleinert 75, 96, Ilya Genkin 76/4, GL Archive 18, Glow Asia RF 3br, 34cr/5, Hemis 66/4, 96tc, Hero Images Inc. 2/6, i love images 17, Image Source 12/2, Image Source Plus 87c, ITAR-TASS Photo Agency 93, Jamie Pham Photography 87l, Robert Kneschke 27, MBI 22/5, Megapress 34r/5, Jeff Morgan 14 95, 96bl, OJO Images Ltd 22/4, 91, Sean Prior 2/5, rgbstudio 12/3, Chris Rout 22/3, RubberBall 100; **Corbis:** Juice Images / Ian Lishman 2/4, KidStock / Blend Images 22/6, Ocean 2/2, ZenShui / Sigrid Olsson 35tr; **Datacraft Co Ltd:** 54/5; **Digital Vision:** 80; **Fotolia.com:** Goran Bogicevic 54/1, CandyBox Images 35cr, chawalitpix 60, Eléonore H 13, 35br, faizzaki 60, feferoni 67b, fergregory 34/3, godfer 34, Iva 76/3, J_Foto 23l, 35cl, Kara-Kotsya 54/4, KaYann 76/1, 81, koya979 34/2, Kzenon 86b, michaeljung 26, Felix Mizioznikov 22/1, napgalleria 34/1, notyouraveragebear 72, PiLensPhoto 67t, 96tl, Andres Rodriguez 9, Sabphoto 12/6, Subbotina Anna 77/1, 83, 96cr, S. White 34l/5; **Getty Images:** André De Kesel 55t; **PhotoDisc:** Ryan McVay 12/4; **Shutterstock.com:** AVAVA 21, Galina Barskaya 4c, Blend Images 48bl, Ross Brown 19, CandyBox Images 9, chungking 76/6, Costazzurra 34/4, Creatista 4lr, br, Robert Crum 23r, 101t, Dim Dimich 14, dwphotos 86t, 96bc, edg 87r, br, 106, Tara Flake 3tl, R. Gino Santa Maria 3tr, Giuseppe_R 4ll, 48tl, pointstudio 90, Dieter Hawlan 61b, Hubis 40t, Ivaschenko Roman 82, mira 61t, John Kershner 104b, Brian Kinney 64t, kouptsova 3bl, majeczka, mangostock 12/1, milias1987 28, Nella 77/5, Nestor Noci 77/3, 96c, rgey Novikov 2/1, 54/6, 64, Odua Images 38cr, Oleg_Mit 38cl, Edyta wlowska 32bl, Pecold 76/2, photogl 12/5, Phon Promwisate 77/2, 96cl, photo79 54/3, Julian Rovagnati 4t, Serg64 99tr, silver-john 103, Slazdi 6, Somchai Som 77/4, 105, Aleksandar Todorovic 76/5, Ian D Walker 78, cy Whiteside 48tr

Cover images: Front: **Alamy Stock Photo:** Ronnie Chua

All other images © Pearson Education

Every effort has been made to trace the copyright holders and we apologise in advance for any unintentional omissions. We would be pleased to insert the appropriate acknowledgement in any subsequent edition of this publication.

Illustrated by
Zaharias Papadopoulos (Hyphen), Q2A Media Services, Anthony Lewis, Christos Skaltsas (Hyphen).

Tracklist

Class CD track number	Workbook CD track number	Unit and activity number
7	2	Unit 1, activity 3
9	3	Unit 1, activity 5
12	4	Unit 1, activity 7
13	5	Unit 1, activity 9
15	6	Unit 1, activity 14
17	7	Unit 1, activity 17
25	8	Unit 2, activity 6
28	9	Unit 2, activity 7
30	10	Unit 2, activity 15
32	11	Unit 2, activity 17
40	12	Unit 3, activity 5
43	13	Unit 3, activity 7
45	14	Unit 3, activity 15
47	15	Unit 3, activity 18
55	16	Unit 4, activity 6
58	17	Unit 4, activity 8
60	18	Unit 4, activity 14
62	19	Unit 4, activity 16
69	20	Unit 5, activity 6
72	21	Unit 5, activity 8
74	22	Unit 5, activity 17
76	23	Unit 5, activity 19
83	24	Unit 6, activity 5

Class CD track number	Workbook CD track number	Unit and activity number
86	25	Unit 6, activity 6
87	26	Unit 6, activity 8
89	27	Unit 6, activity 13
91	28	Unit 6, activity 15
98	29	Unit 7, activity 2
100	30	Unit 7, activity 4
103	31	Unit 7, activity 5
104	32	Unit 7, activity 7
106	33	Unit 7, activity 12
108	34	Unit 7, activity 15
115	35	Unit 8, activity 3
117	36	Unit 8, activity 5
120	37	Unit 8, activity 6
121	38	Unit 8, activity 8
123	39	Unit 8, activity 16
125	40	Unit 8, activity 17
132	41	Unit 9, activity 4
135	42	Unit 9, activity 6
136	43	Unit 9, activity 8
138	44	Unit 9, activity 13
140	45	Unit 9, activity 14